# eco deco

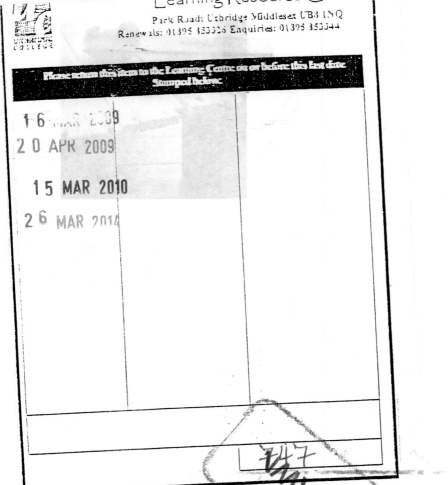

# eco **deco**

## eco-friendly design ideas for the home

stewart and sally walton

APPLE

*To all those wonderful people who saved, sorted and donated their rubbish to us –*
*thanks, we think we've got enough for now.*

This edition published in the UK in 2007 by
Apple Press
7 Greenland Street
London NW1 0ND
www.apple-press.com

ISBN: 978 1 84543 230 0

This book was designed and produced by
Anness Publishing Ltd
Hermes House
88–89 Blackfriars Road
London SE1 8HA
www.annesspublishing.com

Front cover shows Glass & Steel Table – for project, see pages 74–7

### Publisher's note
The authors and publishers have made every effort to ensure that all the instructions in this
book are accurate and safe. They cannot accept liability for any resulting injury, damage or
loss to persons or property however it may arise.

### Diagrams and measurements
The diagrams with the projects include the measurements for the materials that we used when
making up the specific examples that were photographed for this book. These are included
to help you determine the proportions of each piece, rather than as a literal guide to what
you should be buying and making. This book is all about sourcing and using recycled
materials and adapting the projects to suit the materials you find rather than buying new
materials and making exact replicas. When you use recycled materials your version will be
different – it will be yours alone.

### Picture credits
The publishers would like to thank the following agencies for permission to
reproduce pictures in this book:
AKG London p8tl © Succession Picasso/DACS 2000; p8tr; p8br © Succession
Marcel Duchamp/ADAGP, Paris and DACS, London 2000; p9 © DACS 2000.
South American Pictures p10tr. Crafts Council p.28tl.

# contents

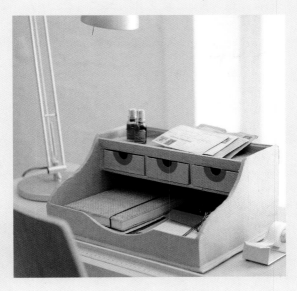

# introduction

*Let's talk trash. The world is overflowing with it, and we have discovered that we can't get enough of some of it. Instead of throwing things in bins or dumpsters, we have started taking stuff out of them. Looking in restaurant windows may make your mouth water, but the place that really gets our creative juices flowing is at the rear, where they throw out the trash. Ah, those rice sacks, fruit trays, oversized cans, corks and bottles – it's like trash heaven.*

**Above** Fruit boxes and old plastic sacks awaiting collection could be turned into decorative and useful items.

**Opposite** An inspired use for a rusty sheet of corrugated metal. This was bent into a curve and irregular crosses were cut into it with an angle grinder. The sheet is wall mounted and lit from behind to project a pattern of crosses. (Chris Richardson)

The idea of using rubbish to create beautiful things is being embraced by young artists and designers everywhere. Released from the preconceptions associated with "proper" art materials, quirky creativity can take over and they feel free to try, free to fail or even free to give up without feeling guilty.

The conventional design process begins with an idea, and then decisions are made about materials. In the world of recycling it usually works the other way around. On discovery of a box of used zips (zippers), one thousand corks or a roll of rubber tubing, the creative juices begin to flow, and in no time you find yourself analysing the material's merits, its strengths and weaknesses and, most importantly, its aesthetic possibilities.

Many designers enthuse about the sense of creative liberation they experience when working with recycled materials. For some, the catalyst was student poverty, but others had always been drawn to brightly coloured packaging, other people's cast-offs or spare parts. Freed from the expense of buying conventional artist's materials, their approach was far more experimental and their work all the more exciting for it. Most insist that they would not exchange their methods or raw materials even if they could afford to do so.

One common complaint from artists and designers was that although their work was much admired, buyers expected to pay lower prices than they would if the materials were brand-new. The designs often take longer to produce and the materials longer to find, but because of their component parts they are still considered to be lightweight, cheap and quirky, even though the finish is fine. And a fine finish is essential. There is little point in designing and making something from reclaimed scrap if the end result looks like rubbish.

Working with recycled, found and reclaimed materials has its own set of constraints, especially when everyone begins with their own version of the required materials, which will depend upon what you manage to find. We hope that the projects in this book will inspire new ideas, not just show how to make exact replicas. Feel free to copy them exactly, if you like, but as free to change them and take them a stage further. In keeping with the philosophy of the book, we suggest using up materials that you already own, and adapt the projects to suit your own equipment, workspace and aesthetic ideas.

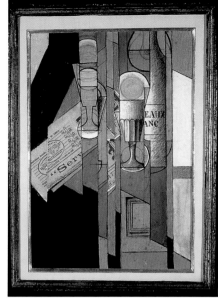

Above *White Bordeaux* by Juan Gris, 1913. Gouache and chalk. Printed bar room ephemera including labels, packaging and advertising leaflets were the trademark ingredients of the Parisian Cubist's collages.

Left *Chevre* by Pablo Picasso, 1950. Picasso's wit and tireless creative genius led him to make sculptures out of every kind of trash material.

Recycling in art has been happening since the early part of the 20th century when the Cubist artists Pablo Picasso (1881–1973), Georges Braque (1882–1963) and Juan Gris (1887–1927) created collages from newsprint, packaging, labels and other found materials. Throughout his long artistic life Picasso assembled found objects to make hundreds of unique sculptures, once simply putting together a saddle and a pair of handle bars to represent a bull's head.

Marcel Duchamp (1887–1968), one of the leaders of the Dada movement, displayed his "ready-mades", including a urinal and a print of Leonardo da Vinci's *Mona Lisa* with a jaunty drawn-on moustache and beard, in art exhibitions in New York. They caused quite a stir then, but his work is now highly respected.

Duchamp gave up art when he was 38 years old and took to playing chess instead. Later Kurt Schwitters and Robert Rauschenberg based their styles on an assemblage of "found materials".

Not all of us aspire to be fine artists, of course, but we are all creative beings, and the environment in which we live reflects this. Interior decorating has never been more popular and the innovative use of unconventional materials is a key feature in modern, creative design. In this book we explore the possibilities of using found, collected and scrap materials to furnish and decorate the home.

Right *Box in a Suitcase*, a ready-made, 1919, by Marcel Duchamp. A suitcase full of odd items, pieces of wire and an image of the Mona Lisa.

**Above** *Maraak, Variation I* by Kurt Schwitters, 1930. Oil and collage. Kurt Schwitters was inspired by all kinds of printed tickets which he collected for his collages. Legend has it that he once chose to miss an important train connection having realized that his ticket was the final component needed to complete a painting.

## Necessity - the mother of invention

Even when you don't have much money you can still have style. And having our pick of all the finest equipment and materials can actually feel inhibiting. A limited selection of recycled materials offers a more liberated creative challenge.

People who live in developing countries have a far greater incentive than those in wealthy Western countries to recycle material. Recycling becomes a necessity, and families spend their lives sifting through rubbish dumps on the outskirts of sprawling cities, collecting cans, bottles and anything else they can reuse or repair.

In Mexico there is a tradition of making colourful tinware from old cans, and everything – from hubcaps to number plates – is used to make useful items for the home. In Morocco steel-rimmed tyres (tires) are cut up and riveted together to fashion elegant water urns, and in Zimbabwe fertilizer sacks are shredded to be woven with grasses into exquisitely patterned sun-hats.

Children in South African townships have been making articulated wire trucks as toys for decades, while their mothers stripped out telephone cables and wove beautiful baskets from the fine, multicoloured wires. Misprinted sheet metal from the canning industry are big business in West Africa, where they are made into briefcases, and in India recycled printed tins are turned into oil lamps, with surface decoration that ranges from cockroach spray to talcum powder.

Western tourists and collectors of folk art have discovered all these wonderful things, and they are now mass-produced for the tourist and export market. The global marketplace demands it.

**Above** A couple making baskets from recycled plastics in Bogota, Colombia.

**Right** This hat was made in Zimbabwe from the strong local bush grass and thin strips cut from farm fertilizer bags. The colours, patterns and finish are quite exquisite.

## Responding to the creative urge

There seems to be less resistance to the idea of one person's rubbish being another person's raw material in the United States. Perhaps this stems from the way the continent was colonized by Europeans, who arrived by sea with what possessions they could carry, and by Africans, who came shackled as slaves with no possessions at all but rich memories of tribal customs, crafts and skills.

There is a long history of recycling in the United States. Early immigrants reused every scrap of material – from the sails of their ships to the clothes off their backs – and eventually passed what remained of them on to their slaves. Even when freedom

came, the slaves were too poor to become consumers, and theirs was a hand-me-down existence. Getting every ounce of use out of materials was a part of everyday life.

Poverty and ingenuity can combine to produce new decorative aesthetics. The belief that Appalachian communities pasted their walls with newsprint because they could not afford wallpaper may have been founded on truth, but the practice evolved into a folk style that was not only decorative but also practical and instructive. Stories were pasted up from which children learned to read. What goes around comes around, and a top New York design studio recently had its floors covered in newspaper then coated with many layers of clear varnish, to complement the 'industrial chic' interior

design style. Americans have a genuine respect for folk art, and the creative efforts of untutored present day artists are applauded alongside those of the past.

The "outsider art" movement is recognized as a genuine expressive art form and celebrated because of the materials used, not in spite of them. The movement shows how the creative force exists across all levels of society, and truly gifted people will find a way of expressing themselves with whatever materials they have to hand. Obsessive collectors of hubcaps, number plates, bottle caps or tin cans created staggering sculptural installations, which rise like shrines to the spirit of creativity, and though often far from the beaten track and with no anticipation of an audience, they now attract thousands of visitors each year.

**Top left** Rick Ladd, the artist who created this mirror, lives and works in New York City. His unique style, known as "bottle cap baroque", is a fascinating blend of furniture and sculpture. Influenced by both folk and outsider art, he is drawn to overly ornamental creations such as grottoes, Burmese temples and sculptural environments.

**Top right** Traditional American quilts frequently used old scraps of clothing. This machine-pieced sampler quilt uses American-block designs including Bear's Paw, Churn Dash and Le-Moin Star.

**Left** Visit architectural scrap dealers and discover an extraordinary range of recycled materials. You need a selective eye as shop signs, old plumbing fixtures, stained glass panels or a set of pine doors will all be jumbled up together.

**Above** A more elegantly displayed selection of outdoor features and furniture.

### The growth of recycling

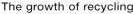

Recycling isn't a new idea in Europe by any means. People have always saved unworn machine parts for reuse in repairs, clothing has always been passed down through families, milk bottles have been returned for refilling, and currency keeps on circulating. In times of war and famine, when supplies of raw materials ran low, people mended and made do, but when peace and prosperity returned those ideas were quickly abandoned. Conspicuous wealth means conspicuous consumption.

In the second half of the 20th century the concept of built-in obsolescence took hold. If manufacturers produce a washing machine that lasts a lifetime, they will sell only one to each customer; if they produce one that lasts ten years, they'll sell a lot more washing machines. As a further safeguard against goods lasting too long, the exterior styling has to change even more often – a new look at least every five years renders that which was most desirable one year, most dated the next.

In Europe and the United States the recycling movement has developed from Green awareness. Overpopulation, industrialization and increased environmental pollution have led to a questioning of consumerist values. Interestingly, this movement is strongest in the wealthier, more sophisticated countries, such as Germany, Switzerland and the Netherlands. It is a doctrine of the "haves" rather than the "have-nots".

In Europe there is more interest in recycled product design than in purely decorative art, and furniture, architecture and innovative recycling in product design is fêted, exhibited and appreciated alongside more traditional art forms.

In Britain children's art and craft activities are often based on the use of recycled household materials, but this may contribute to a negative perception of the value when designers want buyers to take their work seriously. Most of the talented designers listed by the Crafts Council as working in these materials attribute their enthusiasm for the medium to the time they spent at art school. Tutors realize what a great leveller thrown-away materials can be. When poor students compete on equal terms with those who are better off, creative thinking and skilled craftsmanship come out on top.

### Packaging

Once upon a time packaging was simply a way of identifying, wrapping or containing a product to get it from the factory, to the store and to the home. Packaging is now as big an industry as production, and at least a third of every household's rubbish consists of packaging.

**Above** Reclamation yards present us with delightful juxtapositions like these dining chairs, elegant lamps and upturned baths.

**Right** Raw materials stacked up awaiting collection. In Chicago, a scrap dealer, Mr Imagination would race ahead of the sanitation department trucks to sort out the most attractive trash for his artworks.

Products have to compete in the marketplace as they stand alongside their competitors on supermarket shelves. They have to be stackable, storable and highly desirable. A simple hessian (burlap) bag of rice with a price label attached will sell at the style-conscious top end and the frugal bottom end of the market, but in the middle, where most people shop, rice needs to be displayed in a strong, laminated cardboard box that is printed in full colour with a recognizable logo and a mouthwatering photograph of a delicious-looking dish. Once it gets home, the rice goes into a storage jar and the box goes into the bin.

Packaging gets really out of hand in the high-tech market where items can now be made too small to be considered good value, even though they function well. The result is bulked-up packaging, which disguises the item's actual size until we get it out of the box. Most people are not really fooled but still keep throwing away the packaging.

The problem is that we are creating more waste every day and running out of places to put it. Landfill sites fill up, incinerators produce noxious gasses, and pollution of the seas threaten marine life. The throw-away society will soon run out of places to throw things away.

## Can we change the world?

A few decorative projects in a book like this may not be enough to change the world, but each time someone says, "Don't put that in the waste basket – I could use it", or asks their friends to collect plastic bags or tin cans for a project, the seed of the idea of "cool" recycling is planted and begins to grow. Each time a photograph of something smart, wacky and made from scrap appears in a stylish magazine and explains how, why and what was used to make the object, the idea permeates further into our everyday culture.

In the same way that people eventually understood the full implications of the destruction of the rainforests only when the ozone layer was threatened, a time will come when landfill sites begin to encroach on the quality of people's everyday lives and recycling will not seem so much an option as a necessity.

A problem many people have with recycling is that rubbish can be a dirty business. Imagine waking up one morning to find that recycling had become easy overnight and that separate waste sorting bins had appeared along with neat storage systems with compartments for everything that could be reused. It seems like an unlikely dream, but it isn't too far-fetched; all that is needed is an ecologically aware financial investor, a creative industrial designer and a common will to succeed.

# collecting materials

Whether your passion is for brightly printed packaging, weathered misshapen driftwood or plastic bottlecaps, the temptation to add to your collection is not one to be easily resisted. Once you have spotted the potential beauty in an egg carton or olive oil can, it is extremely difficult to pass one by. As long as you have space to store them, it is a case of the more, the merrier.

# collecting materials

A good place to start collecting is in your own home. Stop to think about everything you throw in your waste basket. One of the best ways to do this is to start a compost heap which can take all the non-meat food scraps and leftovers. This is probably not a good idea if you're living in a high-rise apartment in the city, but any home with a garden, backyard or terrace can use compost. A recycling system by which glass is separated from plastic, paper and metal also makes sense. This way you will really be able to see what you've got and assess its potential.

**Left, below and opposite** Small and large businesses often dispose of quite large quantities of materials that are excellent for creating cards, collages and other objects. There is no harm in approaching them to acquire their leftovers.

## In the workplace

It is hard to think of any workplace that does not generate some rubbish that is specific to the activity carried out there. As art students we spent many hours huddled around the hot drinks vending machine, and eventually a clever jewellery design student came up with a range of necklaces and bracelets made from the plastic cups the machine dispensed our drinks into.

A production line will always have off-cuts or scraps, whether the product is a perforated sheet or the actual perforations – either way, something is left over at the end. Where there is quality control, there will always be rejects. Large companies have strict guidelines to prevent the distribution of rejects and off-cuts, but a small business may well be persuaded of the worthiness of your cause. It is always worth asking.

## Scrap projects

If you are lucky and live in an environmentally enlightened area, a community recycling project may be in operation. These schemes collect, accept and sort materials from various sources. They provide materials either freely or for a small fee, and the larger projects handle household furniture, glass, plastics, metals and even building materials. There are other projects that deal only in interesting, reusable, industrial waste.

The projects are usually open to the public, and everything is for sale at a reasonable price to fund the day-to-day running and staffing costs.

There are also recycling depots located all over most countries, run by committed environmentalists and artists whose work is partly funded. They collect scrap materials directly from local factories, which saves on disposal costs, and for a small annual fee offer a choice of materials to people working on non-profit-making educational and community-based projects. Teachers, galleries, community arts organizers and

play schemes all qualify. Anyone who meets the criteria should investigate the network and track down their nearest scrap project.

The one we visited was an Aladdin's cave, filled to bursting with neatly sorted treasure. Drums contained multicoloured computer cables, bright rubber discs, car upholstery off-cuts, plastic flowers, buttons, buckles, plastic sheets stacked up high, and coloured paper and cardboard and many thousands of unrecognizable but highly desirable bits and pieces. Depots from different areas also swap materials among themselves to maintain a good variety of stock.

**Above** Packaging from another country is often more enticing than the more familiar brands we regularly see in our local stores. Never miss a chance to collect printed ephemera. It is perfect material for collages.

**Right** Printers recycle mounds of off-cuts (scraps) and misprinted papers all the time. Explain your project and most printers will be happy to offer you some of their scrap paper.

## Cardboard and paper

Paper is all around us in the developed world. We throw away so much of it every day that all you really need to do is decide which type you need for your chosen project and then to go out and collect it.

Most of the recycled paper products that we now buy are made from high grade paper waste, which comes from sources such as office stationery, paper mill waste and printers' off-cuts. Luckily, papier-mâché is best made from low-grade waste, such as newsprint and telephone directories, whose fibres break down more easily.

Picture framers are a good source of high-quality cardboard and mat board. When framing mounts (mats) are cut, the centre pieces are treated as waste unless an enterprising recycler makes enquiries. Maps, architectural plans, legal papers, flyers and other printed ephemera all make

interesting wall finishes. Small printing firms are worth approaching because they discard a lot of paper in the form of print errors, off-cuts (scraps) and plain newsprint. Printers' waste is usually recycled, but they appreciate fine quality paper and may prefer it to be used creatively than pulped with all the rest. It is always worth asking.

Wallpaper has been made from recycled paper for longer than any other commercial product, but manufacturers deliberately kept quiet about it, thinking that buyers might resent paying high prices for something essentially second-hand. Nowadays we are better informed, and recycled paper has a positive image. Use

rolls of plain or textured wallpaper 'bin-ends' (scraps) on your walls, adding pattern, colour and new textures of your own.

Some of the most interesting looking packaging papers are to be found in foreign food stores or ethnic fruit and vegetable markets. Cast your eyes over the litter after a busy day's trading, and you may discover some gems. Tissue wraps from citrus fruits printed in black, gold and vibrant colours can look fantastic spaced across a white wall. When they are pasted up the white tissue disappears into the background, leaving brilliant medallions of colour. A collection of printed paper bags will bring back memories of happy shopping expeditions.

## Wood

### Old wood

The best source of old wood is broken furniture. Any work environment where matching contract furniture is fitted – hotels, offices, hospitals and schools, for example – have mass throw-outs from time to time. As soon as a certain percentage of the furniture is worn out or damaged, everything is replaced to maintain a coherent style. Second-hand furniture dealers may take the pick of the crop, but there are always leftovers. Befriending second-hand furniture dealers is a good idea in any case, because a lot of their work involves house clearances, and anything deemed unsaleable will be dumped. Let them know what sort of wood you're interested in and offer to save them a trip to the local city dump.

Old houses and apartments are always being stripped out and modernized. Keep a lookout for builders' skips (dumpsters) in the road where old doors, window frames and even occasional floorboards can be found. Remember that you need permission to remove anything from a skip (dumpster), but do ask, for permission is usually granted. It makes good sense for the builders because each item you remove makes room for another and that saves them money.

Also look out for old broomhandles, stepladders and garden implements, but check them for woodworm before bringing them indoors.

### New wood

Packing cases for fruit are made of lightweight, poor-quality pine. Although grocers will sometimes use them to display fruit and vegetables, most are destroyed or dumped. The wood is often printed in bold colours or pasted with bright suppliers' details and labels. If you have an eye for funky graphics, get down to the grocery store and arrange to take spare boxes off their hands.

Good wine is still packed in pine boxes, which are much more solid than those used for fruit. The boxes are imprinted or heat stamped and elegantly labelled. Unlike fruit boxes, these cases are always in demand, but wine warehouses still throw out damaged ones and local storekeepers can always be befriended.

Building sites always have off-cuts (scraps) of construction timber and cable

drums. Scaffolding boards, wooden pallets and floorboards are the real treasures, but never assume that something is unwanted, even if it appears to have been cast aside. Always ask a person in authority and be prepared to be disappointed. The materials may not be theirs to give.

Do not overlook the most obvious source of new wood – the timber merchant. When wood is cut to suit a customer's requirements, a lot of waste is created. The best off-cuts of many types of hard and soft woods including decorative mouldings are usually bundled up and sold at bargain prices, but the smaller oddments are often simply thrown away or shredded.

### Natural wood

Tree cuttings, fallen branches, driftwood or old fencing must be dried before use. Driftwood may be waterlogged from a long sea journey but will have been spared the ravages of insects on the forest floor. Wash driftwood well and leave it to dry out before attempting any drilling or sawing. Check any fallen branches before lugging them home – they can contain a lot of wildlife.

**Above** Collecting driftwood can be a rewarding and relaxing experience and you can make a great variety of items with it, such as mirror and picture frames, planters, small tables and chairs.

**Middle** Pallets stacked as high as skyscrapers could be seen as potential bed bases, shelving or seating.

**Left** Some architectural salvage yards specialize in internal woodwork, such as architraves, skirtings, dado (chair) rails and doors and a proportion of their stock is damaged in removal. Ask about reject pieces which can be ideal for furniture making.

## Glass, ceramics and pebbles

Every household generates a lot of glass waste, especially after entertaining. If you only need one or two bottles or jars for a project then decide upon a shape and colour and adapt your shopping list accordingly. If you need a large number of a certain type of glass, such as blue water bottles, then it is a good idea to find a local restaurant or wine bar that uses your favoured brand and offer to collect from them on a regular basis.

Obviously, greater care must be taken if you are collecting broken glass or china and a good pair of strong suede work gloves are recommended.

Save all china breakages, especially those treasured patterned pieces and ask friends to do the same on your behalf. Visit flea markets, charity (thrift) shops and table sales, keeping a lookout for damaged pieces with good colour and patterns. These will be very cheap as they are of no practical use.

Lids, spouts and handles can be incorporated into broken china mosaics and whole cracked plates can be broken in a controlled manner and used to make circular designs.

Keep a watchful eye for interesting pebbles on trips to the beach. Large quantities should not be taken but a handful of distinctive shapes are fine. Another seaside speciality is sea-smoothed coloured glass, which should always be collected as each piece is a unique treasure. There are strong arguments against removing stone from its natural environment, so let it rest in peace and look for stone at reclamation yards, demolition sites and in skips (dumpsters).

**Bottom left** Stained glass windows, stone carvings and porcelain sinks are standard fare in most reclamation yards. The quality varies and it is worth paying regular visits until you find exactly what you are after.

**Top right** Chimney pots are sought after as plant pots, but are so numerous that there seems to be a never-ending supply in different designs.

**Middle right** Individual marble and granite slabs, slate roofing tiles, glass bricks or pebbles and shells can be combined to make unique pieces of sculpture.

**Bottom right** Stone balusters and glass bricks form a tightly organized display that already looks like art. Four balusters and a sheet of glass would make an unusual and inexpensive table.

## Fabric

Bleaching, dyeing and cleaning our clothes wreaks havoc on the environment and the fashion industry depends on our constantly buying the new and throwing out the old. A massive shift in collective consciousness would be needed to make fabric recycling work on a scale that would make a real difference, but you can make a start by creating something wonderful – so wonderful, in fact, that everyone who sees it wants one the same, and it can be made only by recycling fabrics.

Fleece is a brilliant modern invention: it is a warm, washable, comfortable and extremely lightweight fabric, which is manufactured from recycled plastic bottles. It takes only 25 plastic bottles to make one fleece jacket. Sadly, the home production kit is still a long way off, but fleece garments are certainly worth reusing because the fabric cuts easily, comes in an array of colours and does not fray.

The first place to look for recyclable fabric is in your own wardrobe. After that you need to visit jumble sales (garage sales), charity (thrift) stores and flea markets. Old clothes and furnishing fabrics have always been reused, but the practice was usually associated with a lack of availability or a shortage of money. These are the materials of patchwork quilts and rag and plaited (braided) rugs, which can easily shed their old-fashioned image if you favour a more contemporary approach. Makers are now choosing to reuse old fabrics for their quality alone.

Fine bed linens, embroidered silks and tapestry work can be found in charity sales (thrift stores), and they really do not make fabrics like them anymore. Snap them up whenever you see them. Woollen (wool) garments can be unravelled and restyled if you knit, or felted at hot temperatures if you don't (see Fabric: Felt Penny Rug). Sample books are a good source of upholstery fabric for cushion covers. The pattern and colour ranges change every season and are of no use to the stores once discontinued. You may need charm to acquire them, but it will be worth it.

**Above** Trust your instincts and collect fabrics that catch your eye. Sometimes you will notice a pattern or colour in amongst a pile of old clothes or remnants and these are worth snapping up. They may never pass your way again!

**Top left** Patchwork quiltmakers understand the wisdom of collecting odd pieces of material. For this type of work the weight and texture of the fabric is as important to the design as the colour and pattern.

**Bottom left** Textile mills have spools large enough to double as children's seating and the fabric swatches come in all the colours of the rainbow.

## Plastic

You can easily begin with the home harvest. So much of the food we consume, the containers we buy our beauty products in and the cleaning products we use are packaged in plastic. Buttons, screw tops, shopping bags, cotton reels (spools) and electric flex may one day become the most wanted material for your project.

Binding strips, which feature in one of our projects (see Plastic: Woven Plastic Table Mats), are used to secure large cardboard cartons, such as those used for freezers, washing machines, televisions, hi-fi systems and other electrical appliances. Visit an electrical dealership and ask the storeroom supervisor to save a bundle in a selection of colours. Many of these stores collect old appliances when new ones are delivered, and these can be a good source of plastic-coated wiring and unusual components. A search through your local business directory will identify any small plastics factories in your area. Moulding, laminating and vacuum forming are the most likely factories to be there, but the possibilities are endless. A telephone call or visit to explain your creative motives may be all that is needed to keep you well supplied with some top-class materials.

Also check any upholsterers for vinyl off-cuts, signmakers for perspex (Plexiglas™) and plumbing firms for ducting pipes and tubing.

**Above** When plastic shapes are cut out on a production line, the perforated sheets which remain are of no worth to the manufacturer, but are usually more interesting to the eco-designer that the original component would be. These could be potential curtains.

**Right** A stack of scrap polystyrene tiles, some imprinted with the letters of the alphabet.

**Far right** This roll end of plastic tubing on a large wooden spool looks like sewing thread for a giant. Track down local scrap or waste projects to get your hands on this sort of industrial waste.

## Metal

Cans are either made from aluminium or steel or from a combination of the two, and not many of us will ever manage to reuse as many in art and design works as we get through when eating and drinking. Save the ones you like best and get into the habit of recycling the others. Cans from other countries look more interesting than familiar ones, and catering sizes (oversized cans) are more likely to have the product information printed directly onto the surface. Bring back interesting cans of food as souvenirs of foreign vacations and incorporate them into your metalwork designs, or do it the easy way and shop in Indian, Italian or Chinese grocery stores.

A lot of metal parts are used by the garment industry – zips (zippers), poppers (snaps), hooks, buttons, rivets, pins, chains and buckles might be just what someone is looking for – and when fashions change a lot of waste occurs.

Locksmiths change locks all the time and have thousands of keys. Plumbers install new heating radiators, tanks, boilers and miles of copper piping, and electricians remove old cables and fittings, and all of these are potential materials for the designer who works with recycled materials.

Shopfitters throw out shelving racks, panels and display units all the time, because each time a store changes hands it is completely refitted to attract new customers.

If you are into heavy metal, a car scrapyard is the place for you. Springs, sprockets, spark plugs, exhaust systems, wing (side) mirrors, hubcaps and all the other body parts from which every make and model of car is made can be obtained from a scrapyard. Some yards will be more organized than others, with each part listed and labelled in a storeroom, but the most exciting ones will be piled high with rusting wrecks and you will have to help yourself. This is not for the faint-hearted, but then, heavy metal never was.

Rusted metal has a beauty all of its own and many artists prefer using it to new metal. Look out for rusty chains, spare car parts, garden or farm implements. As the rust advances it softens hard edges in a way that is impossible to imitate. If you want to halt the rusting process, apply a proprietary rust inhibitor, then seal the surface with machine oil.

**Above** A box filled with chrome bathroom fittings, just waiting for the right person to come along.

**Right** Architectural metalwork can mean anything from guttering to garden gates. This yard offers a fine selection of old cast and wrought iron railings, gates, plinths and stacking office chairs.

**Far right** An assortment of light metal fixtures, such as buckles, ring-binders, eyelets and springs, gleam like treasure in a pirate's chest. The material itself is the creative catalyst when you come across unusual bounty like this.

# cardboard and paper

There cannot be many of us who have not already used and recycled paper or cardboard. Designing with recycled paper can be as straightforward as sourcing your preferred material and making something from it, or taking the paper back to the pulp stage and moulding it to create brand-new forms. Surface design presents another range of creative possibilities with ever-changing styles of printed packaging, labels, beermats, luggage tags, advertising posters, wrappers and tickets, all of which make excellent raw materials.

Some of the earliest examples of recycling in art appear in the collage work of the Cubists in the early part of the twentieth century. Packaging, newsprint and even wickerwork were pasted down as part of compositions that were further embellished with drawing and paint. Papier-mâché's history is rich and varied and it appears in the fine and folk art of many cultures. Here we show how artists and designers have used paper pulp in a new way, not to imitate other materials or shapes but celebrated as a medium in its own right.

**Square table** Occasional table utilizing cardboard tubing in a unique "three-way function system" ("Jo Crow Designs"). This system allows for various adjustments and the potential for other furniture designs. (Joseph O'Connor)

**Wastepaper basket** This is made from old advertisements from billboards and hoardings. (Same)

**Papier-mâché raffle ticket bowl** This unusual bowl has been constructed on a base of corrugated cardboard with a curved "collar" to give it sloping sides. The base was coated with layers of blue and yellow raffle tickets, arranged to radiate outwards and make an abstract graphic pattern. Three coats of clear varnish give the bowl its sheen.

**Moulded "Quentin" Lampshade** The vk&c partnership is an innovative Scottish design group which won a prestigious design award for this lampshade. It is vacuum formed from recycled, paper mill waste, and it can be used singly like this or as a module to make up a larger pendent light fitting. Apart from being environmentally sound, the Quentin shade is stylish and radiates a wonderful warm light.

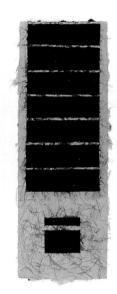

Decorative table This is made from a mixture of paper, newspaper, wood, a covered bicycle wheel, wire and glass. (Lois Walpole)

Abaca rhythm These panels are made from a combination of recycled paper and a material called abaca, which is made from fibres and pulp. The paper is built up in layers and the final one is recycled paper that has been dyed black. They form part of a series that uses geometric shapes for an architectural effect. (Vanessa Godfrey)

Four blue squares Vanessa Godfrey works with paper pulp, exploring different qualities of fibres and the contrasts of fragility and strength that can be achieved by casting or compressing the pulp. For this piece she has dyed recycled pulp with pigments and used a masking technique to create a pattern of waves across the paper.

**Cardboard module shelves** This stacking system is made from recycled cardboard. (Elizabeth Beesley)

**Tomato box chest** This chest was made from combining tomato boxes thrown out by a supermarket and a simple frame. The boxes can be left as they are or painted and varnished. (Andrew Gillmore)

**Circular table** Occasional table made from recycled cardboard tubing. The vertical tubes can be used as "holders" for potted plants or display items. (Joseph O'Connor)

# working with card

Most of us start our creative lives with a sheet of paper and a stubby crayon, held tight in our toddler grip. Paint comes next and then scissors. Cutting, tearing, sticking our way through childhood, we reach "serious school", and for many people fun with paper and cardboard is at an end. Perhaps it is the child within us that relishes the idea of paper pulp or pasted-up strips of newsprint. It is certainly worth a try – it requires no financial input, will occupy many a happy creative hour and at the end you will have a handsome and useful object to brighten up your home. Paint or varnish your finished objects to make them more sturdy.

## Corrugated cardboard

We are all familiar with cardboard as packaging, but you may not have used corrugated cardboard as a craft material before. These simple techniques show the best ways to cut, bend and fix the material to make the most of its strength and durability.

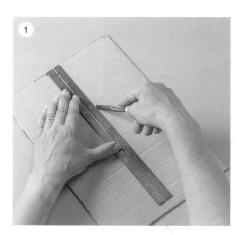

## Folding and cutting

**1** Corrugated cardboard will fold very neatly across the flutes if you score first. Do this by drawing an indented line with a blunt metal instrument, such as the end of a teaspoon handle, guided by a straightedge.

**2** To fold the scored cardboard, hold the straightedge on the line and raise the cardboard up against it.

**3** Corrugated cardboard can be easily cut using a utility knife and a metal straightedge. Place the card on a special cutting mat or a sheet of spare cardboard to protect your work surface.

**4** PVA (white) adhesive – also known as white glue, woodworker's glue and school glue – is the best bonding agent for cardboard and paper. It is milky white when you apply it, but dries clear. To get the best bond, apply a thin coating of the adhesive to both surfaces, then weight them or clip them together until the glue is dry.

## Making paper pulp

**1** To make about 1 litre/1¾ pints of paper pulp for moulding, tear four double sheets of newsprint into small pieces. Soak these in a saucepan with a good covering of water then simmer for about 20 minutes. Allow to cool, then process a cupful at a time in a liquidizer.

**2** Strain the pulp, pressing it down into the sieve to remove any excess water. The mushy paper should be damp but not soggy.

**3** Mix in 112ml/4fl oz of PVA (white) adhesive to add strength to the pulp and prevent the moulded shape from disintegrating.

**4** Colour can also be added to the pulp at this stage – powder paint colour, acrylic paints and inks or dye powder are all suitable colouring agents.

## Scoring and curving

**1** To achieve an evenly curved surface when you are working with corrugated cardboard, score the card first, otherwise it will take up the angles of the fluting. This is done by cutting a row of equally spaced lines through the top layer only on one side.

**2** Once scored in this way, the card is easy to bend into a curve with the scored lines on the outside.

# tools and equipment

**Cutting mat** A self-healing mat marked with horizontal and vertical grids, available from craft and art shops.

**Craft knife** A design and surgical tool with very sharp, removable blades, which is ideal for precision cutting.

**Utility knife** A chunky handle fitted with retractable and replaceable, strong, sharp blades.

**PVA (white) adhesive** A strong, water-based, low odour and inexpensive white glue that dries clear.

**Masking tape** Low-tack, removable tape.

**Wallpaper paste** Dry flakes are mixed with water to form a clear gel adhesive that can be used for papier-mâché. Because it may contain fungicide, wash your hands after use or wear protective gloves.

**Gum strip (gummed paper tape)** Brown paper tape with a dry glue backing. Wet the tape and use before it dries. It is very strong when dry.

# equipment and safety

Every task will be easier and safer to perform if you have the right tools. This is even more true when you are working with reclaimed materials, which have not been specifically prepared for the task you have in mind.

Always recycle paper. It saves trees.

# African-style shelf

If this were a real South African shelf it would be made of mud and decorated with an ever-changing display of brightly coloured magazine pages as shelf-liners. Our shelf is made from papier-mâché on a corrugated cardboard base, and it pays homage to the ingenuity of home makers who have no money to buy materials but who nevertheless create vibrant, attractive and practical furniture and fittings from materials that have no intrinsic value.

Papier-mâché can be made in several ways, but the method suggested here makes a set of strong yet lightweight shelves. The corrugated cardboard base is held together with strong tape, with the more typical covering of layers of newsprint to round off the edges and thicken the shelves.

Choose the top layer of newsprint carefully, mixing some good colours with areas of print. This will give you the option of simply varnishing the unit and making a feature of the base material. We chose various colours of paint – the brighter the better – but another variation would be to paint all the cavities in one colour and the outer frame in another.

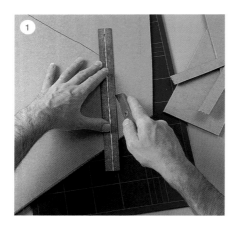

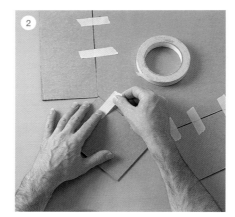

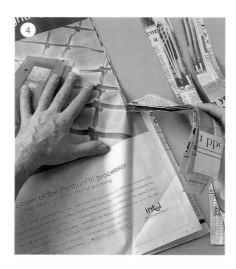

1 Cut out the back following the template at the back of the book.

2 Cut all the other pieces of cardboard to fit onto that shape and assemble the base structure, holding the parts together with masking tape.

3 Insert the section dividers and hold them in place with tape. Add on the decorative scalloped edging pieces of card.

4 Tear the old newspapers into long strips along the grain.

## you will need

corrugated cardboard – a flat piece approximately 800 x 400mm/31 x 15¾in and lots of smaller pieces

template, ruler and pencil

utility knife and straightedge

masking tape

newspapers

wallpaper paste or diluted PVA (white) adhesive or flour and water paste

paintbrush and paint in several colours (optional)

matt varnish

5 Tear the strips into smaller squares across the grain and prepare the wallpaper paste or an alternative glue.

6 Paste and place the old newspaper squares all over the cardboard shape, overlapping each piece with at least half of the one next to it. Take your time smoothing each piece with your finger to squeeze out any excess paste, which would add to the drying time.

7 Aim to cover the base with at least three layers of papers so that all hard edges become rounded. Leave until it is absolutely dry.

8 If you wish, paint the inside nooks and decorative edges in a selection of bright colours. Paint the outer frame a terracotta colour or blue. When the paint is completely dry, apply two coats of matt varnish to protect the surface.

# packaging collage

Paper patchwork is a lot quicker and easier to complete than the stitched variety, and with a few coats of varnish it could be just as long-lasting. To make the most of the packaging graphics, limit the patchwork to four or five of your favourites and arrange them as borders and blocks. We used squares, but other traditional patchwork shapes such as diamonds or triangles can also be used to good effect.

Packaging from far-away places always looks more interesting, quirky, bold and vivid than the familiar home-grown variety. A visit to a specialty foreign food store will reveal a wealth of national characteristics. Japanese packagers favour a different range of colours from their Italian counterparts, and once you begin to take an interest in packaging, a visit to a food store in a foreign country becomes as interesting and exciting as one to an art gallery.

Think of Andy Warhol and his Campbell's soup cans and select your patchwork squares to make a piece of dazzling abstract art.

## you will need

hardboard for backing, 33 x 15¾in

mitre saw

narrow 24mm x 12mm/1 x ½in timber to make the frame cut into:
2 x 400mm/15½in lengths
2 x 840mm/33½in lengths

wood glue and pins for attaching frame

hammer

sandpaper

lots of your favourite packaging – spaghetti wrappers, spice packets, cookie mix, candy wrappers, cornflakes boxes, labels

cutting mat

utility knife

steel straightedge

wallpaper paste

brush

varnish

paint for the frame – we used blackboard paint

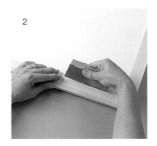

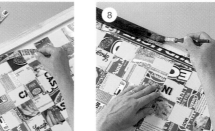

**1** Cut the hardboard for the backing of the collage to the required size. Mitre the edging timber to fit, then pin and glue it down in line with the edge of the hardboard base to make a frame. You can alter the dimensions to suit the size of the frame you require.

**2** Sand the edges smooth.

**3** Using the cutting mat grid as a guide, cut your chosen material for the border into strips 20 x 230mm/¾ x 9in. Cut enough strips to fit the border's length and width.

**4** Cut out a variety of squares for the main body of the collage, each measuring 50 x 50mm/2 x 2in. Arrange, then rearrange all the pieces until you are happy with the design. You can use any kind of packaging or colour scheme you wish.

**5** The wallpaper paste is applied to both surfaces. Paste the base then paste each individual piece and stick down all the squares, leaving a 20mm/¾in border around the edge.

**6** Apply a coat of paste to the border.

**7** Stick down the border strips, trimming them with a craft or utility knife to fit.

**8** Paint the frame using emulsion (latex) paint, choosing a colour from your design or one that complements it. We chose blackboard paint, which gives excellent, one-coat, matt coverage. Once the paint and glue have dried, apply several coats of clear matt varnish to seal and protect the surface.

# egg carton frame

The idea behind this oval mirror frame developed a long time ago when we decided to see how many different things could be made from egg cartons. The daffodil trumpets and petals were already there – all we had to do was notice them. Initially, we had planned to paint the flowers a naturalistic yellow and orange, but the matt white base coat looked so perfect that we kept it. The finished mirror frame has a delicacy reminiscent of fine ceramic, plasterwork or carved marble.

Egg cartons are a perfect example of how recycling should work. Not only are they brilliantly functional and manufactured from pulped recycled paper, but most egg cartons are used more than once. If they are undamaged, people really can see the point in saving and returning them to a local store or market for reuse. Supermarkets demand fresh packaging for everything, but their egg cartons still circulate elsewhere.

Choose egg cartons made from the finest pulp, because the coarser ones are not as easy to cut and shape. The cutting out is a wonderful group activity for a rainy day. It is repetitious but requires very little thought once you have perfected your style. Children are very adept at cutting out. If you have any, then the task will be even easier. Not all egg cartons are made in the same style, so look out for ones that are suitable for this project.

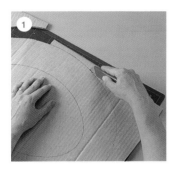
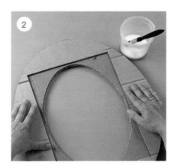
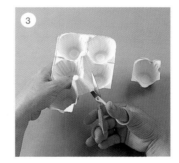
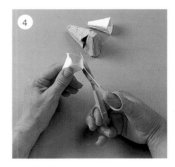

**1** Enlarge the template from the back of the book and cut two shapes out of cardboard.

**2** Cut a smaller oval centre out of one piece and a rectangular shape to hold the mirror from the other. Glue the two together. If you wish, use gum strip (gummed paper tape) to disguise the raw edges.

**3** Cut all the cups from an egg carton, leaving the taller, central parts intact.

**4** Trim the tall shapes to form the flower centres. You will need at least 50 centres. Cut the fluted ends into a pretty frill.

## you will need

template
corrugated cardboard for oval frame base
pen
utility knife and cutting mat
strong glue stick or PVA (white) glue
gum strip (gummed paper tape), optional
egg cartons – a lot of them, mostly white
small scissors
white emulsion (latex) paint and brush
matt white paint – aerosol undercoat
  gives the best coverage
mask
3mm/⅛in mirror glass cut to size
strong adhesive tape

## equipment and safety

Follow the manufacturer's recommended safety procedure when using aerosol paints. Use them only in a well-ventilated area and do not inhale the vapours. Protect the surrounding area by using a large cardboard carton as a spray booth.

5 Cut the cups into five petal shapes. Use the ridges as the petal centres because they look most realistic. You will need at least 50 of these to make daffodils with plenty of petals.

6 Assemble the daffodils by placing two petal sections on top of each other then adding a centre. Each part must be glued firmly in place. We used an extra-strong glue stick for this.

7 Once the glue has bonded the flowers can be moulded into shape by pressing the petals outwards and rounding off the centres, which may be square. Paper pulp can be coaxed gently into shape.

8 Paint the base frame white and leave it to dry. If you use gum strip to disguise the raw cardboard edges, this can also be painted white.

9 Pack the daffodils closely around the frame so that they completely cover the base and some petals overlap it. Leave the glue to bond. To give the frame a white "ceramic" look apply several coats of matt white aerosol (spray) paint using a mask.

10 To fit and hang the mirror, take your finished frame to a glazier and have a mirror cut to fit from 3mm/⅛in mirror glass. Use strong, broad household tape to hold the mirror in the rebate at the back. This can be papered over for a neat finish.

# desk organizer

If using the words "desk" and "organize" in the same sentence is anathema to you, read on. This desk-top organizer has a place for all those stray paper clips, rubber bands and pens, as well as somewhere to keep letters and stamps.

The look is utilitarian, with no attempt made to disguise the brown cardboard and sticky tape construction. There is just a nod in the decorative direction, with red stickers on the drawer fronts. It would not look out of place alongside a bit of Japanese minimalism.

The project is simple enough for an older child to tackle with some adult help with the cutting out. Children enjoy making style statements of their own, and this basic shape could be decorated with magazine cut-outs, paints or other recycled paraphernalia.

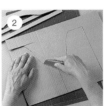
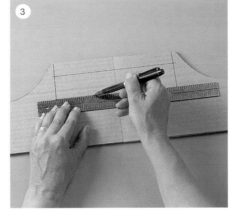

1 Cut out the back and base from the corrugated cardboard in one piece following the diagram.

2 Cut out the sides, front and shelves.

3 Lay the sides on your work surface so that they are back to back and draw lines across both of them to indicate the position of the shelves.

4 Fold the back along the corrugation lines and stick one side in position using gum strip (gummed paper tape).

5 Do the same with the other side and the front piece, setting them slightly back from the edge.

## you will need

corrugated cardboard – for measurements see diagram

straightedge

pencil

ruler

utility knife

cutting mat

pen

brown gum strip (gummed paper tape)

wet sponge

compressed cardboard – such as a shoe box

medium-size coin

corporate seal stickers - available from office stationers or coloured paper

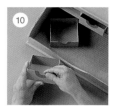

6 Attach two dividers to the base shelf.

7 Stick two shelf ends to the side pieces.

8 Fit the shelf by resting it on top of the two pieces added in step 7. Tape a lip to the shelf edge then neaten the raw edges with a covering of gum strips.

9 Cut the drawer pieces from the compressed cardboard and using a coin as a template, cut a half-moon shape from the drawer front. Use gum strip to secure the drawer together in a neat box shape.

10 If you cannot get red corporate seal stickers you can simply cut a circle of coloured paper and glue it down to highlight the cut-out shape. Stick it on and snip down to the cardboard, then fold and stick the excess over the back to leave a smooth red edge.

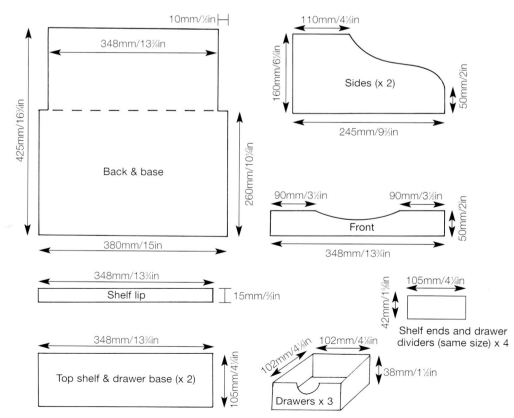

10mm/⅜in

348mm/13¾in

425mm/16¾in

Back & base

260mm/10¼in

380mm/15in

110mm/4¼in

160mm/6¼in

Sides (x 2)

50mm/2in

245mm/9⅝in

90mm/3½in    90mm/3½in

Front

50mm/2in

348mm/13¾in

348mm/13¾in

Shelf lip

15mm/⅝in

348mm/13¾in

Top shelf & drawer base (x 2)

105mm/4¼in

42mm/1⅝in    105mm/4¼in

Shelf ends and drawer dividers (same size) x 4

102mm/4⅛in    102mm/4⅛in

Drawers x 3

38mm/1½in

# wood

Exploring the many types of wooden waste and its suitability for use in the home is both rewarding and useful. Broken furniture is the best source of good quality hardwood and well seasoned softwood, such as ceiling joists, window frames, old doors and stair spindles can be reclaimed from old houses. We are not looking at expensive reclamation, but bits and pieces that nobody else wants. Recycled wood, a few basic woodworking techniques and a selection of tools are all you need to make unique pieces of furniture.

*Wood is a marvellous natural material capable of being worked in so many ways to give such different finishes. The work here reveals some of its potential. Working with recycled wood usually means choosing materials you find locally: driftwood, if you live by the sea; railway sleepers or cable drums if train lines run nearby; old furniture and construction timbers in towns. Every piece has a past and each a story to tell.*

**Wooden boat** A genuine piece of Italian folk art made by a young fisherman. The hull of the boat is a coconut husk, the keel is a lid from an olive can and the sail is a piece of roughly hewn linen. This is art that floats.

**Garden bench** This serendipitous arrangement of well-weathered timber makes a unique and comfortable garden bench. The seat is made from three pieces of old oak, and the backrest is a fabulously smooth piece of driftwood supported on a pair of railway sleepers (ties).

**Wooden shelf** This colourful little shelf unit has been made out of reclaimed fruit boxes and features the original bright colours and bold lettering. The tin lamp, made from a cockroach spray can, comes from India.

**Driftwood lamp base** This lamp was made from a single piece of driftwood, which we found on our local beach. The sea had affected the hardwood in an unusual way, leaving the surface pitted with dark holes. We simply cut the length in half, chiselled out a channel for the wiring, then glued the two pieces together. The brass post for the light fitting has been covered with smaller driftwood pieces, and the base has a wrap of rubber cut from an inner tube.

**Wooden bed** Pallets make an effective and easily assembled bed base for a futon mattress. Be selective when you are choosing – some are painted and stencilled with freight information, which can look good. Four pallets were used here, and apart from a little sandpapering (some pallets may need more sanding than others) to get rid of potential splinters, they were simply pushed together.

**Wooden table** Large wooden drums are used to carry heavy-duty cables, but they also make great garden tables. A power sander was used to smooth the table top, and several coats of clear varnish bring out the character of the grain. These drums are extremely heavy, so be warned – if you find one, arrange suitable transport and help to unload it at the other end.

**Fruit box lamp base** This large wooden table lamp is made from off-cuts (scraps) of construction timber covered with a patchwork of fruit box graphics. The inner timber provides the weight needed, then the box wood is glued and pinned to it. The shade matches one of the colours on the boxes.

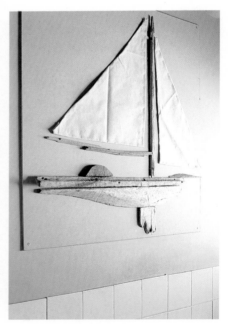

**Bedroom mirror** A full-length mirror has been framed with an assortment of driftwood shapes. The sea affects different woods in different ways, and each piece has undergone its own journey across the sea, encountering many obstacles before it is picked up on the shore.

**Bed head** This patchwork of driftwood forms a huge bed head, complete with pebbles and shells, which have been lodged between the weathered planks.

**Driftwood boat** Calico sails adorn this yacht, which was constructed from a few well-chosen pieces of driftwood. The three-dimensional plaque is well suited to the watery bathroom environment.

**Driftwood throne** Living by the sea, Chris Richardson has naturally gravitated towards the shore and is an avid beachcomber. This giant throne is one of his many creations.

**Driftwood table** A lovely low table, which was made from found wood, bears the scars of its former life with pride. A rough-hewn table like this looks fantastic in a plain, contemporary room. (Chris Richardson)

**Coat rack** Old farmyard timbers and metalwork, weathered by years of good service, and now having a well-deserved rest in their new guise as a much-admired coat rack. (Chris Richardson)

**Thunderbolt (Blue legs)** Kristy Wyatt-Smith's work is part-furniture, part-automaton and part-poetry. This quirky small cupboard is fun to look at and useful too.

**Wooden cupboard** This enchanting cupboard is made from recycled furniture and has practical compartments, a message and a dog, which moves when you turn the handle and appears to be barking at the canaries. The ideas are inventive, but the craftsmanship is superb. Each quirky element is created with a real sense of loving attention to detail which further adds to the pleasure that this artist's work provides.
(Kristy Wyatt-Smith)

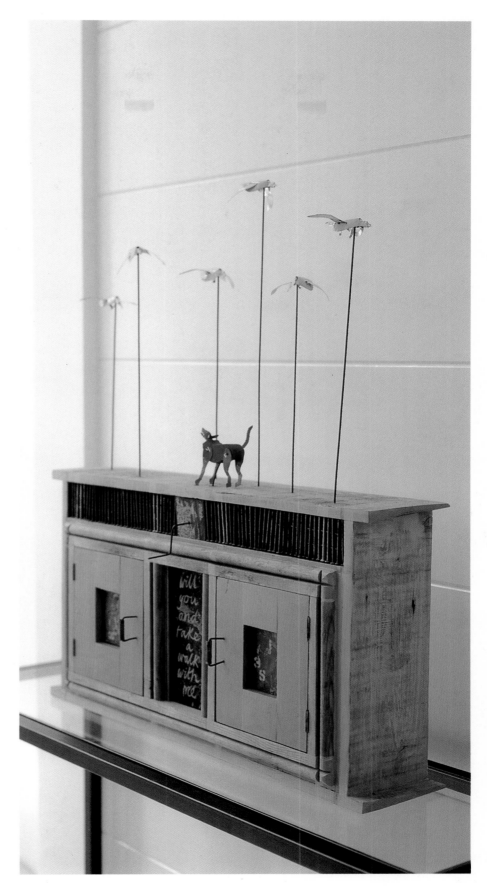

# using wood

There are so many good reasons to use recycled timber. Even fast-growing trees grow quite slowly, and land clearance for their cultivation has a harmful effect on the balance of nature. Using recycled wood may be the only opportunity you have to use some hardwoods, which are now endangered. Old furniture is a rich source of woods such as teak oak and mahogany, and demolished buildings provide pine of a different quality from the pine we grow now. Successful and safe woodworking depends on having a good set of tools, although not necessarily new ones, so keep a lookout for the essentials in markets and second-hand stores.

These basic steps show how to make a bench hook – a useful device that will convert your kitchen table into a workbench – how to construct a butt joint and how to reclaim wood from boxes for use in the projects. We cover particular procedures more precisely where they are needed for the individual projects.

### Making a bench hook

A bench hook is used to support wood while sawing, sanding or paring with a chisel and it will also protect your work surface. It provides a fixed surface to brace against. They are very simple and inexpensive to make.

1 Cut a piece of chipboard measuring 254 x 178mm/10 x 7in and two 130mm/5in lengths of 50 x 25mm/2 x 1in timber. Mark the position of the two pieces of timber on the top-right corner of each side of the chipboard.

2 Knock five 38mm/1½in pins through to the other side of the chipboard.

3 Apply wood glue to one of the pieces of timber, reposition it and knock the pins through into it.

4 Fix the second piece of timber to the other side in the same way. It can be used either way up, with one end hooked under the work surface and the other on the top end as a fixed edge to brace your timber.

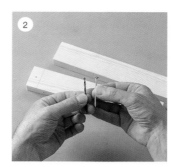

## Constructing a butt joint

A basic butt joint is made from two pieces of wood that are simply glued together, then stengthened with screws, pins or nails.

1 A mitre saw can be set at different angles so that every piece of timber is cut to exactly the same angle. This one is set to 90 degrees to cut timber for a basic butt joint.
The other setting most often used is 45 degrees for a mitred corner.

2 Choose a narrower drill bit than your screw size for drilling a pilot hole. This provides a vertical guiding hole for the screw but leaves enough wood around it for the screw to grip into.

3 Mark the position of the joint with a pencil, place it on a piece of scrap wood and drill the pilot hole.

4 Apply a squiggle of wood glue to the joint. Place the timber on a flat work surface and hold a combination square firmly inside the 90 degree angle while you screw the two pieces together. This prevents the timber from moving with the twist of the screw.

## Recycling fruit boxes

Fruit boxes are stapled together by machine. Dismantle them with the least damage to the wood by following the steps below.

1 Use a small screwdriver and a pair of wire cutters to lift and snip through the wire staples.

2 Ease the staples out of the wood with long-nosed (needle-nose) pliers.

3 Place the reclaimed wood on the bench hook and saw off the damaged ends. Keep the saw blade up against the bench hook to cut at a reliable right angle.

# tools and equipment

**Power drill** Cordless drills are best unless you always use the same workspace. Ask for advice when you buy one so that you get the one most suitable for your work.

**Handsaw** A general purpose saw used for cutting all types of wood.

**Tenon saw** This short saw, with a reinforced rigid back, is held horizontally and used for cutting accurate angles.

**Mitre saw** Used to cut angles for picture framing, mouldings and furniture making. It is accurate and easy to use.

**Jigsaw** This power tool has a vertical cutting blade and can be used to cut curves and follow drawn patterns.

**Mitre block** A moulded plastic or wooden box used with a tenon saw to cut angles.

**Pliers** Both long-nosed (needle-nose) pliers and pincers are useful for removing old nails, staples and tacks.

**Bradawl (Awl)** A traditional wooden-handled instrument for making pilot holes.

**Combination square** A 90 degree set square marked with metric and imperial measurements along one adjustable edge.

**Claw hammer** Use this steel hammer for knocking in and pulling out nails.

**Sandpaper** Vital for sanding down edges. Comes in fine, medium and rough grades.

**Orbital sander** A power tool for sanding rough or painted surfaces. It will save a lot of energy if you are reclaiming wood.

**G-clamps** Simple G-shaped metal clamps screw up to fix wood to a table for cutting or hold two pieces together while gluing.

**Spirit level** To check that your surface is level.

# fruit box frame

Fruit and vegetable boxes are routinely thrown away, even though they are made of light wood. This project springs from our love of packaging and bright, colourful graphic design.

The boxes carry the logos and designs of Mediterranean growers, the names of hot, far-away places, and they are well worth preserving. Once you start looking out for fruit boxes you soon discover a

huge variety of colour combinations and lettering styles. Perhaps a day will come when all these boxes will be made of plastic or cardboard, but until it happens this material is there for the taking.

Show your local grocers what you are interested in and ask them to put some aside for you. Most people love the idea of creativity and are pleased to help, especially if they get to see the finished product.

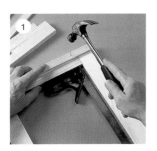

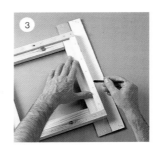

**1** Construct the frame base. Place C between A and B to form a U-shape. Apply glue to joining edges. Glue and veneer pin piece E on top of C along the bottom edge. This secures the sides A and B. Check the inside right angle with a set square.

**2** Do the same at the other end, fitting piece D inside A and B and attaching piece F over the top. Now attach pieces G and H to the sides. They may need trimming to fit – check them against the space they are to fit and make any adjustments.

**3** You now have a frame with a rebate for the backing sheet. Hold the frame against the fruit box and mark off the pieces needed to clad the frame. Remember to include the thickness of the box wood in your calculations where necessary.

**4** Cut the cladding for the front face with a utility knife and straightedge or metal ruler. Take care. Cut with several gentle strokes rather than one hard one.

**5** Mitre one corner of a strip to a 45° angle.

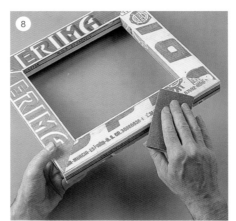

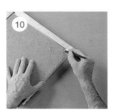

6 Hold this piece in position on the backing frame and mark the mitring points at the other end. Cut this mitre, then glue and pin the first strip in place.

7 Continue this way until all the visible faces including those of the rebate and outer edge are covered.

8 Lightly sandpaper all the edges, taking care not to remove too much of the pattern.

9 Strengthen and protect the surface by adding a coat of clear varnish. This will not change the frame's appearance at all if you choose a matt varnish. If you prefer a more mellow effect, use one with an antique pine tint or use a gloss varnish for a sheen.

10 Measure the back and cut a piece of hardboard to fit. Glass, if used, is cut to the same size as the hardboard. Attach to the frame using swivel hooks or removable pins.

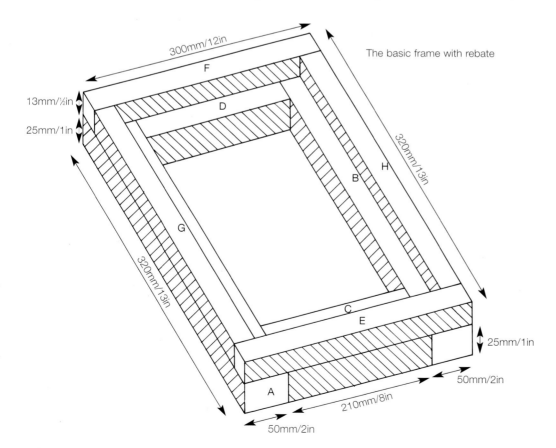

The basic frame with rebate

300mm/12in

13mm/½in

25mm/1in

320mm/13in

320mm/13in

25mm/1in

50mm/2in

210mm/8in

50mm/2in

# driftwood planter

The best time to hunt for driftwood is after a storm, when debris will have been washed up the beach to the high-tide line. This is when the beach is at its most attractive to beachcombers, and if the weather is bad, all the better, because you will encounter less competition for gathering driftwood.

We cannot simulate the shapes and appearance of sea-battered logs and planks, and every piece you find will be unique. Collect an assortment of driftwood, or, if you cannot get to the shore, go to the woods and find weathered broken branches and treat them in a similar way.

Driftwood can sometimes smell unpleasant, so if you intend to use the planter indoors it is best to wash the wood in fresh water and leave it to dry in the sun, before putting it on display indoors. If the planter is to stand outdoors, the rain and wind will do this job for you.

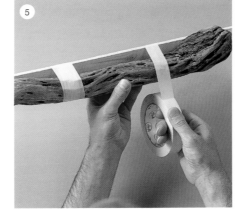

1 Construct a basic butt-jointed frame from the 50 x 25mm/2 x 1in timber. Glue and screw the joints. Glue and pin a 150mm/6in length of 50 x 50mm/2 x 2in timber to each corner. Stand the frame on these legs to glue and pin the feet to the base.

2 Make a mitred frame from the driftwood plank pieces – cut four lengths (see cutting list). Two widths of plank were used here, with inside measurements of 203mm/8in and 215mm/8½in. As long as the angles are mitred at 45 degrees, they will fit together.

3 Glue and pin the frame together then apply a coat of glue to each "leg" and pin them to the frame.

4 Dilute a small amount of white emulsion (latex) paint with an equal amount of water, and brush it on the new timber so that it blends with the sun-bleached driftwood.

5 To cut the oddly shaped pieces to a regular 90 degree angle at the top and bottom, splint each one to a flat piece of boxwood, securing it with masking tape.

## you will need

timber and scrapwood (see cutting list)
tape measure
wood glue
drill
4 screws to attach the butt-jointed frame together and screwdriver
hammer
38mm/1½in panel pins (brads)
nail punch
mitre saw
driftwood (see cutting list)
masking tape
boxwood
wire cutters
white emulsion (latex) paint and brush

## cutting list

collection of driftwood – natural shapes
50 x 50mm/2 x 2in construction timber – you need: 4 x 150mm/6in lengths
50 x 25mm/2 x 1in construction timber – you need: 2 x 300mm/12in, and 2 x 217mm/8½in lengths
4 x 13mm/½in "feet" cut from any scrap timber
Enough driftwood plank (from fencing or pallets) to cut 4 x 350mm/14½in mitred lengths, 4 x 340mm/13¼in lengths of rough plank to clad the base (1 x 13mm/½in scrap timber used here)

**6** Place the pieces in a mitre saw and cut through. Do this to both the ends. Retain all the end pieces as they are used at a later stage.

**7** Slide the driftwood pieces between the two frames and pin them in place leaving about 13mm/½in of the pin standing proud.

**8** Snip off the pin heads with wire cutters.

**9** Squeeze some glue on to each of the pins and press the corresponding driftwood off-cut (scrap) down on to each one. The effect should be that the contorted wood has grown through the plank.

**10** Mitre the cladding timber, glue and pin it on to cover the new base timber and feet.

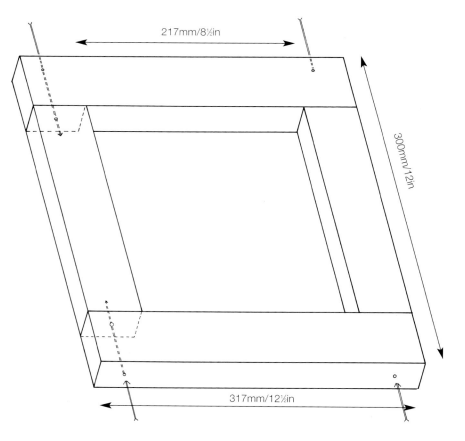

Butt-jointed frame for base of planter

Insert screws here

217mm/8½in

300mm/12in

317mm/12½in

# funky display case

Once all packing crates were made of wood, and no one threw them out unless their damage was beyond repair. Look out for crates like this one made for soup cans. They can often be found in good condition – probably still being put to good use – in your grandfather's garden shed, in older garages or in the storerooms of traditional grocery stores.

The best ones often find their way to antique markets, but they don't cost a fortune – yet. The moulded plastic crates that have replaced them have been designed to hold bottles of specific dimensions, so they are neither as adaptable, or as attractive to recycle with style.

This project is a simple display case given a contemporary edge by the juxtaposition of the three different materials – the smooth, old crate, rough-hewn timber poles and bright new nuts and bolts. For a more practical project, convert the display case into a hallstand with the addition of some strategically placed hooks or nails for your hat, coat and keys.

## you will need

handsaw

4 wooden stakes – fence posts, branches or tree supports

metal file

old wooden crate, wine cases are also suitable

G-clamp (C-clamp)

small scrap of wood

drill

ruler

pen

1m/1yd threaded steel bolt

hacksaw

8 butterfly wing nuts to fit the thread

spirit level

masking tape

**1** To make the legs, saw all four wooden stakes to the same length.

**2** File them to round off the sawn edges.

**3** Decide on the height of the attachment for the box. This can be done by resting it on a shelf or by asking a friend to hold it while you stand back and make up your mind. Clamp the leg, using a small piece of wood in between, to hold it in position.

**4** Drill a hole through the whole of the leg and the box.

**5** Measure the length of the steel thread needed to pass through the leg and the box and to allow some for attaching the butterfly wing nuts on both ends. About 12.5mm/½in extra should be plenty as the threaded steel should not protrude more than 12.5mm/½in from the butterfly wing nut.

**6** Cut a length of thread with a hacksaw.

**7** Remove the burr from the cut end with a metal file.

**8** Fasten the butterfly wing nuts on both ends.

**9** Place a spirit level on the box and use it to make certain that the second front leg fixing gives a level surface inside the box. Drill and bolt as you did with the first leg.

**10** With the box balanced on the two front legs, find the positions for the back legs by placing the spirit level facing front to back on top of the box.

**11** Hold each leg firmly in place – or use masking tape to secure it while you drill through the leg and the box. Bolt the back legs in place so that it stands up squarely.

# cork architrave

Cork is an amazing natural material. It is light, elastic and impermeable, and it grows on trees. It is actually the bark of a species of oak, which grows mostly in Portugal. The trees live for more than 150 years, but they cannot be stripped for the first harvest until they are 25 years old, and after that are stripped only every nine years. The forests are diminishing while the demand for corks increases. Plastic and reconstituted corks or screw-top bottles are unpopular with some wine consumers, who associate cork with quality.

We love corks from a purely aesthetic point of view for the incredible variety of marks, logos, numerals and symbols that have been designed to fit onto these small objects. Once you become aware of them, it becomes virtually impossible to throw them into the waste basket with the scraps. Ours must be a common anxiety, because no sooner had we mentioned that we were collecting corks than we were inundated with them. It was as if everyone we knew had been waiting for a reason not to throw them away.

In this project we made a decorative architrave to go on a wall, but there is no need to stop there – a dado (chair) rail, a picture rail, a pelmet or even a floor could be given a cladding of corks. If you make the architrave described here, fit the strips and corner pieces and then hold them in place with panel adhesive.

 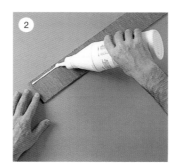  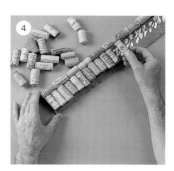

1 Measure the space where you want the architrave to go and cut three lengths of plywood – one to go over the top and two for the sides. Also cut two squares, each 80 x 80mm/3¼ x 3¼in, for the corner pieces. Sand the edges smooth.

2 Begin with the piece that fits over the door. Run a line of glue along the top edge.

3 Lay corks end to end, slightly overlapping at the edge of the plywood, to cover the entire length of the strip. Make the most of the graphic images on the corks as you do this.

4 Add a wiggle of glue down the centre of the strip, then lay corks at right angles to the first row, placing them close together.

## you will need

tape measure
plywood strips for base material
handsaw
sandpaper
wood glue
lots of corks
mitre saw or block
pencil
ruler

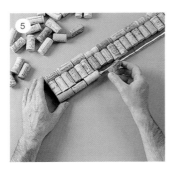   

**5** Complete the strip by gluing another row of corks, this time placing them end to end, along the other edge. Now make up the two long strips in the same way.

**6** To make the corner pieces, work on the squares of plywood. Use the mitring saw to cut a 45 degree angle off the end of 8 corks.

**7** Cut three corks in half using the 90 degree cut on the mitre saw.

**8** Find the centre of the base by drawing intersecting lines from the corners.

**9** Glue one of the half corks so that it stands up in the centre.

**10** Glue two corks on the vertical and two on the horizontal axes to form a cross shape.

**11** Glue four more half corks on end in each section.

**12** Frame the corner piece using the mitred corks. Then leave the glue to bond for two hours. Use these square pieces on the corners or to punctuate any long lengths of dado (chair) or picture rail you make up.

# glass and ceramics

Some people cannot leave a beach without filling their pockets with shells or stones and see frosted fragments of smooth coloured glass as jewels. They are probably the same people who save broken pieces of decorated china. If you are one of them, then this chapter will hold the most appeal for you. Not all of us have access to a kiln or fresh clay and here we show how found materials can be combined in fresh ways that will satisfy both the collector and designer in you.

*Glass and ceramic are hard, sharp and brittle materials that demand a degree of stamina from the designers and artists who choose to use them as base materials.*

*The work here shows how the shedding of preconceptions about these materials can lead to some interesting design solutions and original artworks.*

**Breeze blocks** A simple but effective shelving system has been made from five breeze blocks and two long white planks. Concrete features in the work of many contemporary architects and designers, and this is an inexpensive way to get the look, especially if the blocks are left over from building work.

**Tiles** A plain white wall is the perfect setting for these tiles. The crackling, colour mixing and the depth of the glass create the impression of islands surrounded by blue seas seen from high up in the atmosphere. (Andrea Peters)

**Milk bottle lamp** These are original and useful. The light fitting is made using a halogen light bulb and the wire sits snugly around the rim of the milk bottle which is filled with material to weight it down. (Ralph Jessop)

**Teapot lady** Old galvanized baths and bowls have been decorated with ceramic chips cut from broken china, a couple of old teacups, and ginger-jar tops.

**Mosaic garden wall** A random, growing mosaic made from accidental household breakages meanders around the side of our garden pond. The china is set into a waterproof combined adhesive and grout, which is rubbed with a mixture of garden soil and pond water to blend the new with the old. The occasional seashell is permitted, but the majority of the pieces once graced our dining table.

**Mirrors** Andrea Peters makes tiles, bowls and mirror frames out of scrap glass. She has developed a process to enable her to melt down the original glass and turn it into a new object. The wonderful watery glass is made by using a mixture of pulped paper and clay to make moulds, which burn off during the firing process. The blue, green and clear glasses blend as they melt, and every piece cools to a unique pattern.

**Bottle-shaped lamp** Made from recycled glass, this lamp is one of a small batch of design pieces by Tejo Remy. (Same)

**Victorian table** This charming and intricate mosaic of inlaid broken china depicts a windmill on the octagonal table top and four windmill sails on the lower shelf. The china pieces are small and of extremely fine quality, dating back to around 1870, and it was probably made as a pastime project by a wealthy Victorian lady.

**Slate curtain** These shards of blue slate were rescued from the demolition of a hospital and former Victorian workhouse in Mary Hooper's home town. The piecing together of these fragments is symbolic of healing. Mary is responsible for a visionary arts project based at the new hospital, where she buys and commissions original artworks for display in all areas of the hospital. (Mary Hooper)

# using glass & china

Stones pummelled against each other over thousands of years eventually become grains of sand and, melted at extreme temperatures, sand becomes glass, or when it is compacted in the earth, eventually turns to clay. Clay is shaped and baked to give us ceramics. All these materials are of the earth and will one day naturally degrade to become a part of it again. Our reuse of ceramic pieces, glass bottles and collected pebbles, shells and stones just delays the inevitable.

In the projects described in this chapter we avoided suggesting anything that might prove dangerous, such as smashing glass, melting it or drilling holes in large stones. All these things are possible, as some of our gallery pictures suggest, but it is essential that you have proper equipment and facilities. Look for courses if you want to take your work a step further.

## tools and equipment

**Glass cutter** A small, pen-handled cutter with a rolling blade scores the surface of glass or ceramic tiles. Pressure on the scored line causes a clean break. A matchstick below the scored line and finger pressure from above will snap a tile neatly along the line.

**Glass etch** A DIY (do-it-yourself) aerosol spray will simulate sand blasting.

**Hacksaw** Fine-toothed blades are suitable for cutting ceramics and glass.

**Work gloves** Protect your hands with strong gloves when handling broken glass.

**Goggles** Always wear safety goggles when you are cutting or drilling ceramics or glass.

**Power drill** Ceramics can be drilled with masonry bits and stones can be drilled with tungsten carbide bits. Wear protective goggles.

**Combined adhesive and grouting** For small areas of mosaic, use the pre-mixed type of adhesive and grout, but it is far more economical to mix your own adhesive and grout separately when large areas are to be covered.

**Two-part epoxy putty** Use this to stick ceramic pieces together, or to add surface decoration, such as shells or pebbles.

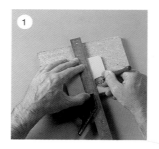

### Cutting and drilling ceramics

1 You can cut ceramic tiles into smaller pieces or trim broken corners with a simple glass cutter and a straightedge. Run the glass cutter along the same line, applying light, even pressure so that you graze the glazed surface.

2 The tile can be snapped cleanly along the line by placing it over the edge of a flat piece of wood and holding it down firmly with a metal straightedge and applying quick pressure from above with the base of your hand.

3 Ceramic jars and bottles, such as this Italian container for rose hip syrup, can be converted into unusual lamp bases if you drill a cable hole near the base. Place an overlapping cross of masking tape at the point where the hole is to be drilled. Fit a masonry bit to the drill and hold the drill vertical. Start slowly and gradually increase to full speed.

### Decorating ceramics

Terracotta pots can be painted with any water-based housepaint or artist's acrylics. The paint used here is a water-based Mediterranean paint, which dries to a chalky bloom. The best style for terracotta is bold and ethnic, with repeated dots, stripes and squiggles or bands of colour. The colour may fade outdoors, but the effect is neither unattractive nor undesirable.

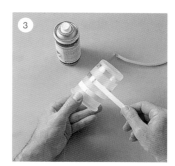

## Decorating glass

1 Contour paste (contour leading) is a thick acrylic paint, which is applied to glass straight from the tube. It is available in a range of colours and hardens to seal off areas of glass for glass paint. The long nozzle can be cut at an angle near the end to give a thin line or further up for a thick one. Unless the glass is already defined by fluting, it is best to place a paper pattern inside the glass or to use a chinagraph (china marker) pencil to draw a pattern on the surface, which can then be covered by the acrylic paste.

2 Contour paste hardens after about 30 minutes and glass paint can then be applied with a brush to fill the defined areas. This glass has been patterned in the style of a Moroccan tea glass, and the pattern creates an illusion of fluting on the plain, curved surface. Do not overload the brush with glass paint or bubbles will form as it dries. Colour can be intensified by another thin application once the initial coat has dried.

3 Genuine frosted glass is produced by sand blasting or acid etching, but several products can be used to create the effect at home. We have used an aerosol version, which is applied in light drifts of spray. Simple bands of paper were wrapped around a plain glass and held in place with small dots of removable adhesive. We used a wooden stick inside the glass to support it and applied the spray sparingly. The contrast will be obvious as soon as you remove the paper masking. Practise on small areas before tackling a window or glass door.

4 A steady hand and the right brush are essential if you are handpainting on glass. Glass paints come in both water-based and oil-based versions, and each type has its own good qualities. Water-based paints are less expensive and fast drying and have a low odour. Oil-based paints give the deepest, richest colours and are longer lasting, but they require solvents for thinning and cleaning off mistakes and brushes. A paper pattern can be placed inside the glass or the strokes can be applied freehand. Experiment on milk bottles or picture frame glass.

# glass & steel table

Throwing wine bottles into the bottle bank can be a terrific way to relieve stress, but this project will give a longer lasting sense of satisfaction. The table is both elegant and practical and the effect of light passing through the glass shapes is quite stunning.

Each pair of bottles is joined at the neck with a cork so that it resembles a giant egg-timer. They are placed close together in a frame of galvanized metal corner brackets. These brackets were part of an abandoned shop fitting and similar ones can be found on basic workshop shelving systems. Similar galvanized angle brackets are used in house construction to neaten

corners before the final skim coat of plaster is applied. We tried several different methods of securing the bottles together but this was by far the best looking and most stable. If you cannot find any metal brackets to recycle, then we suggest buying them new or making a simple wooden box frame from recycled construction timber.

The table top is an unashamedly brand-new sheet of safety glass with smooth edges. Don't risk using anything but toughened glass on a table top and if in doubt ask a glass merchant to check that the glass you plan to use is safe for a table top.

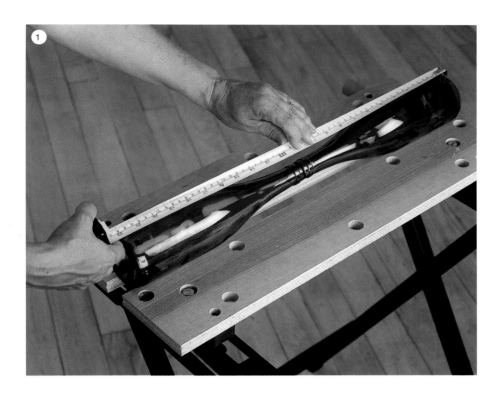

## you will need

18 wine bottles – they must be the same size

tape measure and ruler

5m/16ft of galvanized steel corner brackets from industrial shelving system

vice or Workmate

hacksaw

file

plywood for base

sandpaper

drill and 16 round-headed machine screws and flat nuts

pliers

screwdriver/adjustable spanner for bolt tightening

9 corks and glass cloth

6mm/¼in table glass 300 x 300mm/ 12 x 12in, with ground safe edges

4 clear plastic self-adhesive buffers

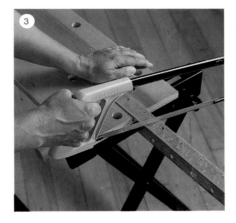

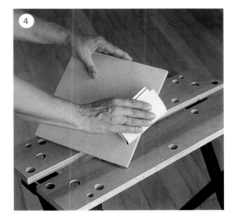

**1** Wash out the wine bottles and dry them. Remove any labels. Lay two of the bottles on a flat surface, butted up against each other, and measure their combined length.

**2** Place three bottles upright and measure their combined width. You now have the dimensions for the base square and the height of the frame.

**3** Hold the bracket firmly in the vice and cut the eight short lengths of metal for the top and base of the table and the four uprights for the sides. File the ends of the brackets.

**4** Cut the plywood base square to match the measurements of the shorter lengths. Sand the edges well to make them smooth and safe.

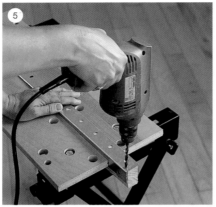

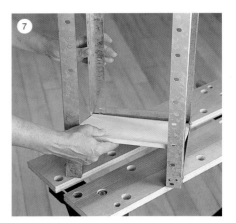

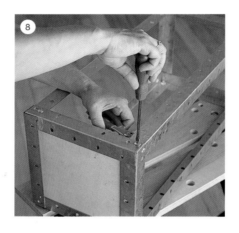

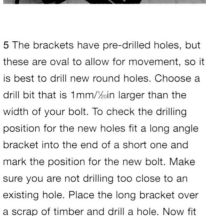

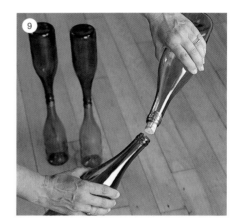

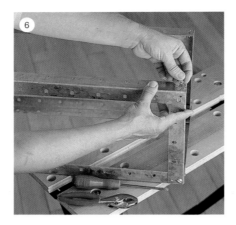

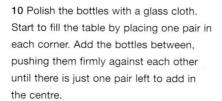

5 The brackets have pre-drilled holes, but these are oval to allow for movement, so it is best to drill new round holes. Choose a drill bit that is 1mm/1⁄20in larger than the width of your bolt. To check the drilling position for the new holes fit a long angle bracket into the end of a short one and mark the position for the new bolt. Make sure you are not drilling too close to an existing hole. Place the long bracket over a scrap of timber and drill a hole. Now fit the short bracket inside it and mark, then drill another hole. Do this for all adjoining corner pieces.

6 Secure the brackets together with the machine screws and nuts. Make up the rest of the frame in the same way.

7 Before fitting the final bracket to the base, slide the square of plywood base into position. It must fit flush against the bracket base below the bolt attachments.

8 Fit the last bracket and tighten up all the bolts using pliers and a screwdriver.

9 Join the bottles together by fitting a cork halfway into each neck and pushing them up tightly together.

10 Polish the bottles with a glass cloth. Start to fill the table by placing one pair in each corner. Add the bottles between, pushing them firmly against each other until there is just one pair left to add in the centre.

11 Place one plastic buffer on each corner and lower the glass top into position.

# concrete tiles

Concrete may not immediately strike you as a recyclable material, but this book is also about using up leftovers, and anyone who has used sand and cement to mix concrete at home will testify that there is always a third of a bag left over, no matter what quantity you initially required. This remains in the shed and hardens with time to become a heavy boulder needing to be disposed of at the local rubbish dump. What a waste of energy and materials.

We suggest that you use the leftover concrete mix to make a set of personalized tile squares. The project described here can be used as a guide and adapted to suit your needs. Experiment with different textures –

one of the best we found was a sheet of clear perspex, which gave a smooth finish that we could not have predicted. It feels so unlike concrete.

The most difficult part of the project is waiting for at least three days before removing the shuttering. Because we are impatient, we did try to shorten the time, but the tiles broke as we picked them up. We advise that you try to forget about them for a week – the wait will be worth it. The materials given here are sufficient to make four tiles, each 200 x 200mm/8 x 8in. You need three times more sand than cement. Wear gloves and break up any lumps in the cement, which must be a smooth powder to mix evenly.

## you will need

plywood and construction timber (see cutting list)

mitre saw

pencil

drill and 12 countersunk screws

squares of galvanized mesh (chicken wire)

wire cutters

straightedge and utility knife

perspex (Plexiglas™)

assorted decorative bits – shells, cardboard, bubble wrap, sea glass

sand and cement

PVA (white) adhesive and trowel

## cutting list

plywood for base of mould – shuttering ply is ideal, cut to 475 x 475mm/ 19 x 19in to make 4 square tiles

2 x 475mm/19in lengths

3 x 430mm/17in lengths

2 x 200mm/8in lengths of 25 x 25mm/1 x 1in construction timber

1 Cut the 25 x 25mm/1 x 1in timber to the required lengths. We used a mitre saw which guarantees regular 90 degree angles.

2 Lay the framing timber on the base and outline its position in pencil. Drill through each piece then screw the frame together. These holes are countersunk, but use the materials you have to hand as this is simply a mould to be discarded later.

3 Cut the mesh to make four squares, each 190 x 190mm/7½ x 7½in.

**4** To cut a sheet of perspex (Plexiglas™) keep its protective paper in place, measure and mark a square 190 x 190mm/7½ x 7½in, then score a line with a utility knife.

**5** Position the line along the edge of a length of timber and apply firm pressure to snap the perspex along the scored line.

**6** Using the perspex as your template, cut out a square of bubblewrap. Place the bubblewrap (bubbles facing upwards) into one of the squares of the frame.

**7** Cut a square of the cardboard. Place the perspex and the cardboard (corrugations upward) into different squares.

**8** Make the cement, using three parts sharp sand to one part cement. Mix PVA (white) adhesive into water, in the proportions of 20 parts water to one part glue, and add it to the dry mix. It should be thick but pourable. If water pools on the surface and it is too runny, you can thicken it by adding a little more cement at a time.

**9** Add the cement to the moulds, pushing it into the corners. Tap and drop the frame to make sure all the air escapes and all moulded parts are filled.

**10** Press the mesh squares down into the cement so that it is just covered.

**11** Press your pattern pieces into the wet concrete. This is easier for pieces that are to remain embedded, such as shell or sea glass. Use the trowel to make ridges on the tiles that have the pattern moulds (cardboard, perspex and bubblewrap) on the base. Smooth the top surface of the remaining square with a trowel.

**12** Wait from three days to a week before removing the tiles. Unscrew the shuttering and lift the wooden dividers off. Peel off the perspex, bubblewrap and corrugated cardboard and leave the tiles to dry for a further two days before laying them.

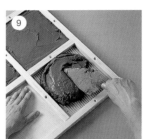

# mosaic table top

Never throw away your favourite china when it gets chipped or broken. Instead, give it another chance to shine as one of the patterns in a mosaic. Unlike a jigsaw, the pieces don't have to fit, because as long as they are nearly the right shape the spaces can be filled by the grout, which frames each shiny piece with a matt, white border. Patterns, colours and shapes can be mixed at will, but a table surface should be level, so use pieces of similar depth or place whole tiles within the pattern so that you can stand drinks on them.

The design here is random, with just four types of ceramic used, but the same technique could be used to make a formal pattern or spell out a name. The best way to approach a mosaic is just to begin. Buy a small pot of ready-mixed combined tile adhesive and grout and cover a flowerpot or a brick with broken pieces of china. It is a perfectly paced activity – you work quickly at first, spreading the base and pressing in your pattern before it sets, then take a break for a half hour or more to allow the adhesive to bond. If you don't have time to complete the next stage, it can wait until you do. The grout is applied all over the mosaic, and is then wiped off with a sponge, so that it remains in the cracks between the pieces. That's all there is to it.

## you will need

chipboard for base – 400 x 400mm/
   15¾ x 15¾in

handsaw

50 x 25mm/2 x 1in timber for the frame or
   use any other edging material

mitre saw

wood glue

pins and hammer

hardboard or thick cardboard the same
   size as the chipboard base

cutting mat and craft knife

straightedge or metal ruler

PVA (white) adhesive

mosaic materials – terracotta, cracked
   and broken china and tiles (we used
   clay pots), a chipped orange mug,
   2 spotted plates and 2 tiles left over
   from the bathroom

old towels

tile adhesive

tile grout

sponge

clean dry cloth

paint and paintbrush

clear varnish (optional)

1 Cut the chipboard to make a base of the required size for a table. Mitre the timber to make a frame to surround the base. Glue and pin the frame. There must be a recess of about 50mm/2in depending on the depth of the material you are using for the mosaic.

2 Cut a matching piece of thick cardboard or hardboard to use for planning.

3 Paint the chipboard with PVA (white) adhesive, diluted with an equal amount of water, to seal the base.

**4** Place large pieces of china or pieces of clay pot between two old towels.

**5** Smash the china with a hammer. This can be done in a controlled way to get the shapes you need.

**6** Plan the layout of your design on the hardboard or cardboard. The design can be whatever you choose – ours is a random pattern.

**7** Coat the board with tile adhesive to give a layer 5mm/¼in deep.

**8** Transfer all the pieces, bedding them down in the adhesive to hide the different thicknesses and to make the surface as level as you can.

**9** Leave to dry overnight, then mix and apply the grout.

**10** When the grout begins to dry, wipe off the excess with a damp sponge.

**11** When the grout is dry use a dry cloth to buff up the shiny ceramic surface.

**12** Paint the frame, using a colour that complements the mosaic, and apply two coats of polyurethane varnish if it is for outdoor use.

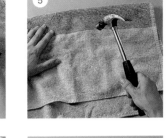

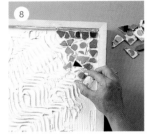

# fabric

The appeal of a certain type of fabric is entirely a matter of personal taste. Some of us go for vivid colour and pattern while others choose a particular weave or weight of cloth. Old shiny damask or silk, intricate lace panels and fine embroidery are heaven to some, while others light up at the sight of nylon, polyester and Crimplene. *Vive la différence!* The fashion industry makes sure that there are mountains of scrap fabric in the world, more than enough to keep us all happy.

*Fabric probably has more potential for recycling than most materials, yet we throw away millions of tonnes of textiles every year. The finest examples of creative work with recycled fabrics often come from impoverished or remote peoples and cultures, who reuse what they have out of necessity. Never miss the chance to examine old appliquéd quilts or rag rugs closely. They were made by ordinary people who had no aspirations to be artists, yet they are truly inspiring because they confirm that the ability to create something beautiful is a gift we all share.*

**Striped velvet cushion cover** Real velvet has the look and the texture of pure luxury, but it has become expensive to buy. The way to get the real thing is to buy old velvet ribbon or strangely shaped dresses from charity (thrift) shops or jumble sales (garage sales). The cushion cover was made from a moth-eaten, purple velvet dressing-gown bought in a sale, a bag filled with off-cuts of gold velvet ribbon and a small remnant strip of red. The dressing-gown's satin lining was used to make the back of the cushion. The secret lies in alternating the raw-edged fabric with rows of ribbon. The ribbon is placed on top of the fabric and stitched using a close zigzag or satin stitch, and as the ribbon edge is sealed, there is no risk of fraying on the right side.

**Black leather and chrome chair** The chair began life in a 1950s kitchen, when it was upholstered in blue and grey vinyl, which had seen better days. We rescued it with the help of a black leather coat from a charity (thrift) shop and some new chrome studs. The chair back was easily unscrewed and re-covered using small black upholstery tacks to secure the leather neatly. On the base we used the most attractive seaming from the back of the coat to define the shape of the seat, and once again it was held in place with small tacks. To finish off the chair we added a row of decorative chrome tacks around the edge of the backrest and re-attached the original maker's tag.

**Shrink to fit** Three of Ben Hall's witty denim hooked rugs, which feature pairs of jeans apparently dissolving into a whirlpool of blue fabric.

**Thumb print rug** Ben Hall makes rag rugs from old denim jeans. He works on a background of old coffee sacks, prodding and hooking strips to make these magnified fingerprint shapes. Ben is a textiles graduate who has resisted commercial mass-production, even though his work is in demand. His motivation is a deep concern for the unemployed, particularly the mining communities in the north of England. He uses denim because of its origin as workwear for manual labourers. (Ben Hall)

**Blanket throw or rug** A soft blue double blanket, found in a thrift shop, inspired the making of this unusual throw, which could double as a rug. The huge blanket was cut in half, and one of the pieces was cut in half again. The next step was to machine-wash the two smaller pieces, one half on a hot wash and the other at a low temperature. This resulted in a subtle change of colour. The blanket was stitched back together, alternating the blue areas. Smaller patch decorations and stitched circles were added.

**Eco Collection** This is a beautiful range of interior accessories and soft furnishings made by Annasach using recycled textiles, and includes knitted woollen cushions, throws and tweed cushions. One of Annasach's aims is to make a serious impact on environmental sustainability in the sourcing of materials. (Stephanie Damm)

**Bath mat** This hand-rolled felt carpet is an ideal bathroom mat. It has a traditional design on the underside and the top pattern is made up of woven fleece. (Victoria Brown)

# working with fabric

Like cooking, sewing can seem complicated if you have never been taught how to manage the basic ingredients – needles, thread, pins and patterns – or how to control a sewing machine.

Fabrics such as silks, cottons and velvets behave in different ways when they are cut and stitched, but with practice and patience, anyone can learn to master the basics, and these techniques will enable an absolute beginner to handle fabrics with confidence. Finding fabrics is tremendously satisfying. After some practice you see riches where you previously just saw rags. Charity shops, jumble sales and thrift stores are not to be resisted as they provide a rich harvest of old clothes, curtains, table and bed linen which can be cut up, perhaps dyed, then woven or sewn to make something unique and wonderful.

## tools and equipment

**Scissors** Small, sharp pointed scissors are used for unpicking and detaching trimmings. Large, stainless steel bladed dressmaker's scissors are needed for cutting lengths of fabric.

**Pinking shears** These have strong, aligned sawtooth edges, which prevent fraying.

**Cutting wheel (Rotary cutter)** The very sharp cutting tool is useful for cutting out patchwork shapes or really thick woollen (wool) fabric. It is used with a metal straightedge.

**Pins** Keep sharp dressmaker's pins to hand.

**Tape measure** Use a tape that is marked with both imperial and metric measurements.

**Cutting mat** The self-healing mat is marked with various grids and is an ideal cutting surface.

**Sewing machine** The one you have inherited will probably be fine for your needs. New machines are lightweight and multi-functional.

**Needles** Get a pack of new needles in a range of sizes.

### Binding edges

**1** Raw edges of fabrics such as satin and velvet fray easily and can be difficult to machine-stitch. Lengths of velvet ribbon can be used to join pieces together in a less bulky way than folding over double seams. This method also allows you to make small remnants of lovely fabric go further. Use a small zigzag stitch along the ribbon edge.

**2** Bias binding is a useful way to extend a limited amount of fabric because it allows you to stitch close to the edge and not turn any precious fabric under as a hem. Lay the opened binding along the edge of the right side of the fabric and machine-stitch down the first fold.

**3** Turn the binding to cover the raw edge of the fabric, pin, then hand hem stitch the folded edge to the back of the fabric. The narrow piped effect can be worked in matching or contrasting binding to enhance the design.

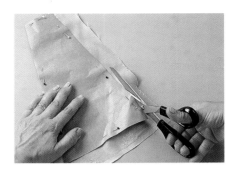

## Joining fabric

No-sew bonding tape can be used to hem fabrics. Fold over a hem with tape inside and simply iron to bond the two surfaces together. Some brands of tape have a paper backing so that they can be ironed on to one surface at a time. The tape can then be stripped away to leave the adhesive on the surface, and this is useful when adding decorative trimmings or patches. The bonding strip also seals the fabric edges and prevents fraying.

## Cutting fabric

1 Pinking shears cut fabric to leave a sawtooth edge that is less inclined to fray than a straight edge. This is particularly useful when you are working with a limited amount of fabric because it dispenses with the need for turning over double seams.

2 Cutting wheels are best used with a straightedge ruler to cut through thick fabrics or many layers of fine fabric. They are extremely sharp and can cut straight lines more accurately than a pair of scissors. They are especially useful for cutting patchwork pieces. When "harvesting" fabric from garments for re-use, it is a advisable to cut away all the zips (zippers) and buttons and unpick any darts and pleats. The fabric can then be washed and pressed.

## Preparing to stitch

If you have the time it is best to tack (baste) two pieces of fabric together before machine-stitching. This will give greater accuracy than pinning and will guarantee a neater finish. Use a contrasting coloured thread and large stitches that can be easily pulled out once the fabric has been machined together.

## Making a paper pattern

It is always worth making a paper pattern if you have more than one matching shape to cut out. This holds truer than ever when you are working with remnants or a limited supply of fabric recycled from clothing or curtaining. Check your measurements and cut patterns from brown paper so that no fabric is wasted.

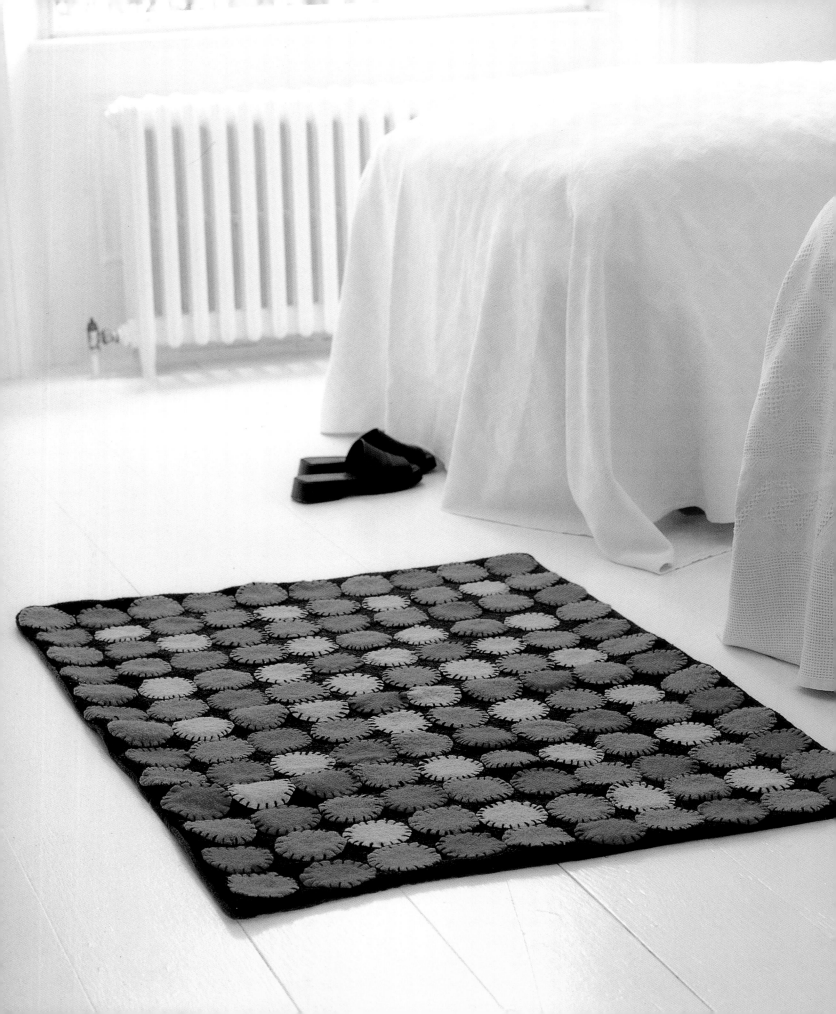

# felt penny rug

Felt has many good qualities, but one of the most useful is that it can be cut and will not fray. This allows for all kinds of creative possibilities, and the felt we have used here is homemade, which is even more thrilling. This style of rug used to be called the "penny rug", and it dates back to the early 19th century in England, when they were made from old suiting fabric and widely used as table runners.

To make felt, you need some old machine-knitted sweaters, a washing machine and a tumble dryer.

The sweaters can be plain or patterned, but ideally they should be of similar thickness. The first stage is to cut up the sweaters, removing all the seams and buttons. Next, add a cupful of washing detergent and put the pieces into the washing machine on a boiling hot wash.

Follow this with a long, hot tumble in the dryer and prepare to be surprised. Hot washing will have softened the colours, and the heat turns the knitting into lovely, soft felt.

## you will need

4 worn-out pure lambswool sweaters, machine-knitted and the same thickness

old single blanket

cotton bedcover for the backing

packet machine dye for natural fabrics

card (card stock) for template

paper for patterns

scissors

pins

fabric glue

ball of dark wool

darning needle

sewing machine

1 The rug described here requires four sweaters. Cut away all the stitched seams and the buttons, keeping the buttons for another project. Wash the knitting on the hottest cycle, then tumble dry on hot. Place the blanket and cotton bedcover in the machine and dye them dark blue, using a machine dye and salt for fixing, according to the manufacturer's instructions.

2 Decide on the size of your "pennies" and make a card template, then cut out paper patterns. These are 75mm/3in in diameter.

3 Pin the paper patterns onto the felt and cut out discs.

4 Lay the circles out on the dyed blanket, spacing them evenly until you are happy with the colour arrangement, using pins to keep them in position.

5 Put a small dot of fabric glue under each one to hold it in place.

6 Thread the needle with a length of dark wool knotted at the end. Insert the needle from below, bringing it up in line with the edge of a disc. All other stitches are worked from above the fabric.

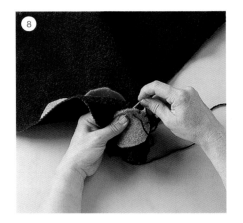

7 Insert the needle, coming up to make a straight stitch about 10mm/½in in from the edge of a disc.

8 For the next stitch, slant the needle about 10mm/½in across, bringing it up in line with the first one. Continue spacing the stitches evenly around the disc, then move on to the nearest adjacent disc, carrying the wool (yarn) over to it.

9 As each length of wool (yarn) is used up, oversew once to secure it, then re-thread the needle to continue sewing all the discs to the background.

10 Cut the cotton fabric to the same size as the backing blanket and hem the edges with a zigzag stitch. Place the backing and blanket together, right sides facing, and pin together.

11 Machine stitch the two pieces together around the edge, leaving an opening for turning.

12 Cut a slit up to the stitch line at each corner so that the excess fabric overlaps and gives a neat flat corner when the rug is folded inside out. You could snip away the excess material. Hand-stitch the opening.

# blue and white squab cushion

This novel idea transforms ordinary tea towels into a wonderfully comfortable padded seat. The crisp white and blue colours are evocative of the seaside, and they give a truly fresh feel to these generous cushions.

This technique is used on mattresses in many countries, such as Greece and Turkey, where they are often filled with cotton or natural horsehair. However, a cheaper and just as effective alternative is wadding or cotton bump. Once you have made your cushion, experiment with it: use it indoors or outside, or why not make a few cushions and stack them on a window recess or on a conservatory bench to make an inviting seat?

You can use tea towels of any design or pattern, but make sure they suit the colour scheme you are working within. Use good quality cotton for the best results.

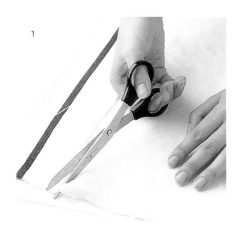

**1** Cut one tea towel down to your required size. This will form the base of the cushion cover. The other tea towel forms the top and sides.

**2** Pin and tack a thin layer of wadding to the wrong side of both tea towels.

**3** Put the tea towels right sides together and join the top section to the bottom section. Leave a gap open at one end so it can be filled with wadding.

## you will need

2 cotton details

scissors

dressmaker's pins

needle and tacking thread

wadding

matching cotton thread

150mm/6in pieces of embroidery thread

quilting needle

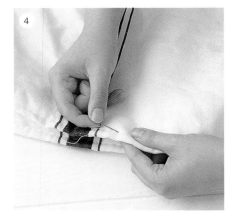

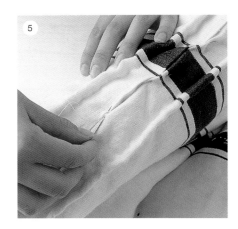

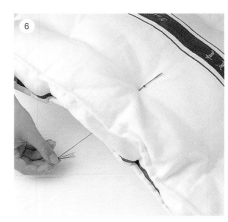

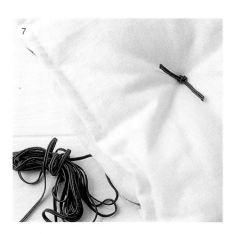

**4** On the right-hand side, make a seam allowance of 15mm/⅝in by pinching 25mm/1in of fabric into a raised section. Pin, tack and fill the cushion with wadding and sew together with a running stitch.

**5** Fill the cushion with wadding and stitch the opening closed.

**6** Mark the positions of the quilting pionts on the tiop and bottom of the cushion. Double knot the embroidery thread at the end and thread it on to a thick quilting needle. At each of the marked quilting points, thread right through the cushion.

**7** Double back the thread through the cushion and knot again. Fix decorative knots on the top with a small stitch.

# brocade duvet bolsters

Big bolsters impart a touch of the exotic, especially if the fabric used is a richly embroidered satin brocade. These long, round cushions were very popular in the 19th century and were considered the height of decadence, and artists such as Ingres painted pampered beauties reclining on low couches, languidly propped up on bolsters.

You don't have to live the lifestyle depicted by Ingres, but why not recline in sensuous comfort from time to time? If this is a look that appeals, get out a saw, cut down the legs of the bed and go curtain hunting to make yourself a bolster.

The brocade fabric used here was a single curtain found in a second-hand store, and the filling is a rolled-up single duvet that had become rather tired and flat. Yes, that tired old duvet does have a use. Roll it up, add a few stitches to stop it unravelling, and you have the makings of a large bolster.

## you will need

single duvet – polyester is fine

thread

tape measure

paper for patterns

single brocade curtain or fabric from an old evening dress

compass

tassles or braid if you have them – curtain tie-backs include both braid and tassles

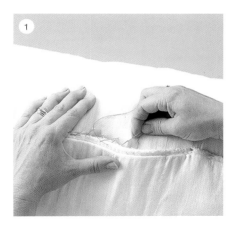

1 Roll up the duvet, either lengthways or sideways, depending on which length you want the bolster to be. Use double thread to sew around the rolled ends and along the long edge. Large tacking (basting) stitches will be sufficient to hold the duvet together until the cover takes over.

2 Measure the circumference of the bolster, adding a further 50mm/2in. Measure the length, add another 50mm/2in, then cut out a rectangle of the covering fabric.

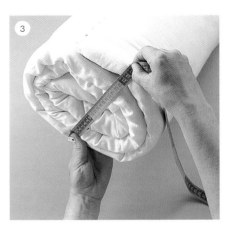

3 Hold a tape up to the end of the bolster to measure the diameter, add 50mm/2in, and halve the total to find the radius.

4 Use a compass to draw out a paper pattern. Cut out two bolster ends.

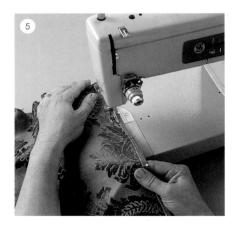

5 Turn the fabric inside out and join the long seam. Start stitching at one end and stop about halfway along. Start again at the end, leaving a section in the middle open for turning and filling.

6 Pin the circular end pieces in place and stitch the seams together. Turn the cover the right way round and feed the rolled up duvet into it. It should fit snugly.

7 Stitch up the open seam by hand, using thread that matches the fabric.

8 If you wish, hand-stitch braid around the end seams and, if you are using tassels, stitch them firmly into the centre of the ends.

Sleeping bags make good bolsters, but any hard metal zips (zippers) should be removed before they are rolled and stitched.

# re-upholstered chair

Few fashion garments date as quickly or entirely as those made from animal skins. One year it's fashionable to wear clothes plain and straight; the next year jackets are smart; then they're flared, fancy or multicoloured. Leather is not easy to alter, and once garments become dated they can be picked up for next to nothing in flea markets and charity (thrift) shops. The leather is often good quality and makes fabulous upholstery material. Details, including shaping and seaming, lend themselves to the shapes of chair backs and seats. Sheepskin coats are often too heavy to wear, but they convert into deliciously comfortable seat covers, and suede simply begs to be stroked.

Look out for 1980s-style jackets. This was the decade when brilliant-coloured leather coats were all the rage, and if you come across a set of cheap chairs in need of an awakening, the padded shoulders and tapered arms may be just the thing to plump up your chairs – and a pocket on the backrest could come in very useful for the TV remote.

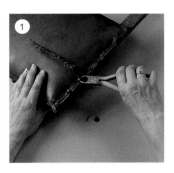  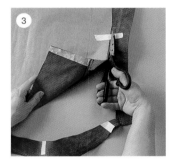 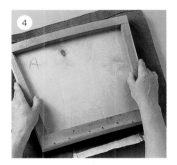

1 Remove all the damaged upholstery material and the staples or tacks that secured it.

2 Place the paper over the parts of the seat to be covered and make patterns to correspond with the shapes.

3 Experiment to find the best section of the garment, then tape down the paper and cut out the shape, adding a seam allowance of 25mm/1in all round.

4 Place the seating material face down on a flat surface and position the seat on top of it, checking that any seams are in the right place before you begin the stapling.

## you will need

chair – choose one with upholstery that is tacked, not sewn

pliers

brown paper for a pattern

masking tape

leather cast-offs – we used a short sheepskin jacket and a suede mini-skirt

staple gun

small hammer

upholstery nails in chrome, brass, bronze or black

scissors

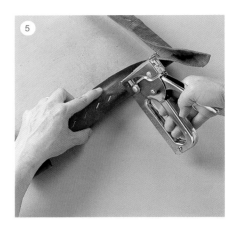

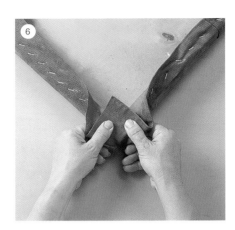

**5** Staple one side in the centre, then pull the leather taut and staple the opposite side. Do the same on the other two sides, then staple all the sides, working outwards from the centres towards the corners.

**6** At each corner fold the leather inwards to create a mitre. Pull taut to fold the excess inside and fold the seam ends flat. If the leather is very bulky the corners can be cut off instead of being folded.

**7** Staple the folded ends to the frame as neatly as possible.

**8** The sheepskin backrest is stapled in the same way. Secure it at four points first to get the tension right, then add more staples. Once this has been accomplished, add an evenly spaced row of upholstery nails.

# plastic

The ability of this entirely synthetic material to be moulded to any required shape has led it to be one of the most useful manufacturing materials, and also one of the major polluters of our planet. Plastics are now collected and recyled on a large scale, but with billions of tonnes of the material being produced each year, there is still plenty of waste plastic available for creative use by artists, craftsmen and designers.

*Everyone using plastic in their art and design has started with the feeling that a material that appears to be so intact simply cannot be discarded as rubbish. The imaginative work shown here becomes all the richer when we realize that the materials have no intrinsic value. The profusion of plastic waste has given artists the freedom to experiment whilst incurring little or no cost, so enabling them to understand the qualities of their chosen material. Plastic has now achieved the status of a "serious" art material.*

**Woven fruit basket** The maker of this colourful plastic basket helps to run a recycled scrap project. She has a background in textiles but experiments with other materials. The arrival in the store of multicoloured plastic bindings led her to create this and other lovely containers using ethnic basketry techniques. The small rubber discs that hold the ends firmly in place are off-cuts (scraps) from scuba diving masks. (Gigi Griffiths)

**Wire basket** Telephone engineers in Zululand, South Africa, used to complain about the difficulties they had keeping the phone lines open when the wires disappeared as soon as they had installed them. The reason eventually became clear, as the demand for these fabulous woven bowls grew and grew. The fine, multicoloured wires are tightly woven in intricate herringbone patterns, and these days the recycled materials are obtained in a more conventional way.

**Egg basket** We bought this little yellow, red and black striped basket in Crete, where it was simply woven from plastic-coated copper on a wire frame. The uneven, homemade quality gives it its charm.

**Rubber basket** A delightful basket made from old rubber tyres. (Idonia van der Bijl)

**Joseph's curtain** Mary Hooper is a conceptual artist whose work reflects the recurring theme of memory and the passage of time. The framework for the curtain is the clear plastic that links six-packs of drinks (beverage) cans together. The colourful fabric and tin discs inside the plastic frame were collected over 20 years. They are saved fragments of her own and her children's daily lives. (Mary Hooper)

**Lampshade** Made from recycled plastic, this bright lampshade is a stylish and colourful addition to any interior scheme. (Same)

# using plastic

Plastic is a fantastically useful and completely recyclable man-made material. Problems arise when non-biodegradable plastic is dumped in landfill sites. If we recycled our household plastic it could be used over and over again, saving money, fuel and the environment. One of plastic's most attractive qualities is the way the material is coloured. Colour is an ingredient rather than an afterthought, and coloured plastic can be opaque, semi- or completely transparent. There is a type of plastic to suit every design specification, whether it is soft, hard, brittle, pliable, light, heavy, smooth or textured.

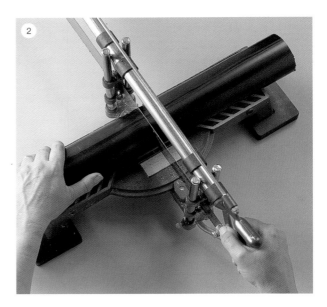

## Cutting plastic

1 Tin shears have sprung handles, which make them an ideal tool for cutting through thick and awkwardly shaped objects, such as this washing detergent container. Pierce the container first, then insert the lower blade and snip away.

2 Rigid PVC, like this drainpipe, is best cut with a saw. To be sure of cutting across the pipe in a straight line, brace it within a mitring jig and set the saw angle to 90 degrees.

3 Plastic shopping bags can be cut into strips with a pair of ordinary scissors. Place the bag on a flat surface and slide the open blade up from the bottom to top edge. Using the scissors in a conventional way will create a more jagged edge.

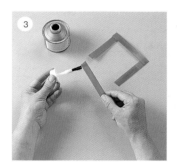

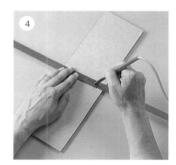

## Stripping flex and joining plastic

1 Electric flex usually contains three strands of plastic-covered copper wire, which is both strong and decorative. To strip the flex, place the flex on a cutting mat and slice it open carefully with a craft knife to strip out the wires.

2 A pop rivet is a neat way to join two pieces of rigid plastic, like this drainpipe and PVC container. Drill a hole through both pieces, insert the rivet and washer and apply pressure with the pop riveter to secure the attachment.

3 Different grades of plastic require particular glues to bond them together. The one being demonstrated here is an extremely strong, solvent-based glue, which is capable of bonding binding tape together and even rigid tubes and drainpipes. It is best to ask for advice from a hardware or DIY (do-it-yourself) store so that you use a glue that is best suited to the materials you are using.

4 Strips of strong plastic, like this binding tape, are best joined by melting the two pieces together. This can be done with a pyrography iron, which leaves a neat, small hole, or a soldering iron, which melts a small slot.

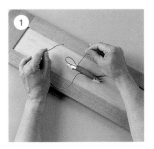

## Whipping

1 Form a loop at one end of a length of wire and lay it flat along the surface of the handle. Begin binding the handle, working towards the loop but leaving a "tail" of wire protruding.

2 When the handle is fully covered, thread the end of the wire through the loop and pull it tight.

3 Hold the end of the wire and pull the "tail" at the other end with a pair of pliers. This pulls and tightens the loop inside the whipping, with the end of the wire also hidden neatly inside. Any excess wire can be trimmed back to the edge of the whipping.

## tools and equipment

**Tin snips** A small pair of snips is useful for making small cuts, such as when cutting plastic-coated wires, flex and cables.

**Tin shears** These are bigger than snips and have spring-loaded handles for easy cutting. The bottom blade is serrated to improve grip and make cutting through thick, moulded plastic easier to manage.

**Riveter** A riveter enables you to attach sheets of thick plastic to other surfaces such as metal or wood. It can also be used for other materials. A DIY (do-it-yourself) user's riveter will have slots for up to four sizes of rivet. They are inexpensive but extremely effective tools.

**Power drill** If you are using a riveter a power drill is essential because rivet holes must be pre-drilled. Plastic is drilled with wooden bits.

**Mitre saw** This complex-looking piece of equipment is used to cut angles, as we did in our tube lighting project.

**Adhesives** Plastic is most successfully bonded with strong, solvent-based glues, which give off noxious fumes and are anything but ecologically sound. Use them sparingly and with great caution – always wear a breathing mask and dispose of the leftovers with care.

# woven plastic table mats

Some materials seem to send out a creative challenge, and plastic binding strips definitely fall into this category. They come in a range of bright opaque colours and black, as well as in translucent shades, like this shimmering green. The material is used in all areas of industry, particularly to secure packaging for deliveries, and it is extremely strong. In warehouses the strips are joined using friction – apparently the heat created melts and bonds two lengths together.

We experimented with all kinds of bonding agents, but nothing seemed to work. We knew that melting them would hold them together, but the problem was how to heat the inner, joining surfaces without melting the top ones. Our results were untidy until we tried using a pyrography iron, which left a small hole, but one that was neat enough to be decorative. A soldering iron is a similar tool and could be used instead.

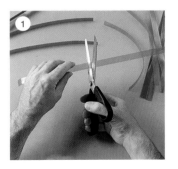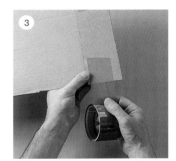

1 Use strong scissors to cut 16 strips of binding, each 250mm/10in long.

2 Cut a rectangle of corrugated cardboard 350 x 250mm/14 x 10in and two strips, each 45 x 25mm/1¾ x 1in.

3 Use adhesive tape to attach a cardboard strip across each end of the large piece of card, so that the edges are held together. This is the "loom".

4 Arrange eight pieces of plastic binding lengthways so that both ends of each strip are held in place beneath the cardboard strips at each side.

## you will need

plastic binding strips of the sort used
  to secure large cardboard packaging
  around electrical appliances such
  as refrigerators

strong kitchen scissors

corrugated card

ruler

adhesive tape

a pyrography tool (plug-in heated spike)
  or soldering iron

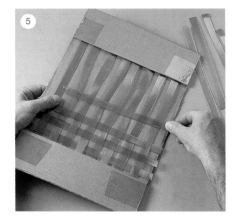

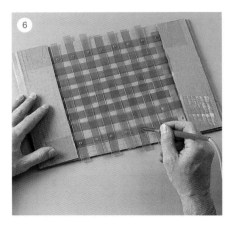

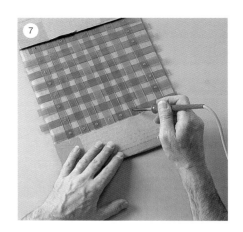

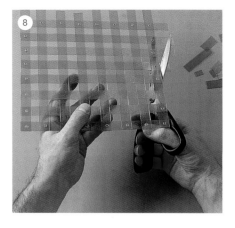

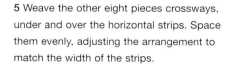

5 Weave the other eight pieces crossways, under and over the horizontal strips. Space them evenly, adjusting the arrangement to match the width of the strips.

6 Heat the pyrography iron. When it is hot pierce each of the overlapping side strips at the top and bottom while the mat is still held firmly in the card loom. As the holes melt, the two layers are fused together.

7 Repeat this process along the two sides. Push down as you do it so that the two surfaces are in close contact as they melt together.

8 Remove the mat from the cardboard loom and use strong, sharp scissors to carefully trim away the excess and neaten up the edges.

# plastic tube light

An experiment with Christmas tree lights and a length of tube led us to design this table light. The shape allows it to be free-standing, but variations on the theme could include an illuminated picture frame, coloured strips of light along a wall or a staggered group of pillars of light. Christmas tree lights come in a wide range of styles, from moving patterns, to multi- or single-coloured bulbs and simple plain light bulbs.

The great advantage of using Christmas tree lights is that they generate so little heat. They have to be safe enough to remain lit – sometimes for days on end – while they are in contact with other plastics, wood, fabrics and the drying branches of a fir tree. If ever a product has stood up to a rigorous test, this is it. We thought that if the lights could cope with those conditions they would be perfect in our plastic tube.

Rolls of any sort of material need a central core, and although these are often made from thick cardboard, some products in the plastics industry are rolled onto strong plastic tubes. We discovered these semi-opaque tubes in waste material outside a builder's yard. The tubes form the core of rolls of the thick plastic that is laid beneath flooring to prevent damp from rising up into the brickwork of newly built houses.

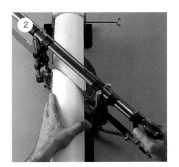

1 Set the mitre saw at 45 degrees. You will need three equal lengths, so measure and mark the tube into thirds, then clamp a block of scrap wood to the mitre jig to restrict the tube to that distance.

2 Push the end of the tube up against the block and cut the first mitre.

3 The central section is mitred at both ends, so flip over the tube and cut the second mitre at the other end. The other two pieces are mitred at one end only.

4 Drill a hole near the base of one of the uprights for the wiring.

## you will need

mitre saw
industrial waste tube of opaque or
   clear plastic
ruler
drill
hacksaw
fine sandpaper
plastic welding solvent glue – do not inhale
breathing mask
Christmas tree lights

## safety

Follow the manufacturer's instructions for using the glue carefully and do not inhale the fumes.

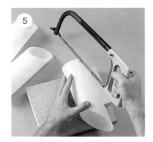

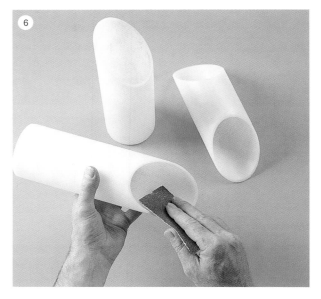

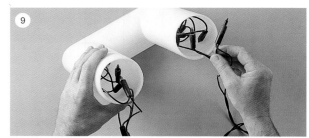

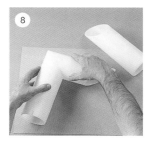

**5** Cut through the base up to the hole so that the wire can slide in.

**6** Remove the swarf (rough bits) with fine sandpaper. Clean the tubes inside and out while they are still unattached.

**7** Place the tubes on a flat surface and apply a coating of solvent glue to the top edge of an upright tube and one of the sides. Hold together for a minute or two, then leave for 20 minutes to bond.

**8** Repeat this for the other side of the light.

**9** Feed the Christmas tree lights through the tube, plug in and admire.

# tubular stool

Garden hoses have the frustrating habit of developing kinks and twists, which block off the water supply just when you are farthest away from the tap. After years of to-ing and fro-ing to unkink the hose and rejoin the connection, the day will eventually dawn when you invest in a brand-new hose and consign the old one to the garden shed – for who can bear to actually throw out a hose that, apart from those few frustrating kinks, is in good condition? This project was inspired by a little stool we spotted in use at our local hardware store. One of the assistants had used drainpipes and a piece of plywood to construct a sturdy, lightweight stepping stool so that he could reach the highest shelves.

We combined a length of leftover plastic drainpipe with our kinky redundant hose to make a safe, sturdy and comfortable stool for a young child. A table could also be made following the same instructions, but you would have to increase the dimensions and omit the hose cushioning.

  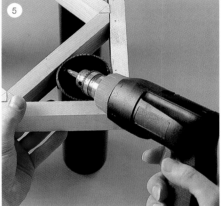

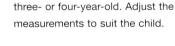

1 Cut out four pieces and butt joint a frame of the 50 x 25mm/2 x 1in timber. Apply glue to the adjoining edges then drill and screw them together.

2 Cut the drainpipe to four equal lengths on a mitre saw. Ours are 240mm/9½in, to suit a three- or four-year-old. Adjust the measurements to suit the child.

3 Cut the internal support struts (see diagram). Mark the centre of the timber end, then mitre in from each side so that the struts meet at this point.

4 Attach the legs to the frame by drilling through the drainpipe and screwing the plastic to the outer frame.

5 Drill and screw the legs to the inner support struts at three points.

## you will need

wood for seat: 300 x 300mm/12in x 12in square

wood glue

drill

38mm/1½in screws

plastic drainpipe, about 1.2m/4ft of 65mm/2½in diameter

ruler

pen

mitre saw

wood for four supports inside: inside measurements of diamond shape: 165mm x 165mm/6½ x 6½in

outside measurements of diamond shape with corners mitred off 200 x 200mm

hardboard, about 300 x 300mm/12 x 12in

hammer

nails

garden hose

utility knife

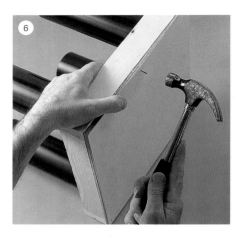

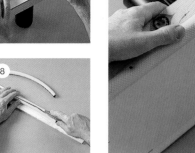

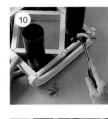

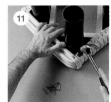

**6** Attach the hardboard to the top, pinning and gluing it to the frame below.

**7** Place a length of hose on the top of the stool, mark the length, then cut two lengths the same size.

**8** Split these with a utility knife and fit them over the top, hard edge of the frame on two opposite sides.

**9** Cut six lengths of hose to cover two opposite sides. Secure each length with a nail positioned about 25mm/1in from the corner. Wrap the hose tautly around the corner and flat along the side edge and around the next corner. Nail the other end down 25mm/1in beyond that corner. Keep the hose taut and fit bands of three closely together.

**10** Cut two lengths of hose that are long enough to wrap over the top of the stool and meet underneath. Use one at each end to cover the exposed nail heads from the previous step, securing them to the underside of the stool with nails.

**11** Cut 13 equal lengths of hose to cover the top of the stool. Position them close together and nail each one to the underside of the frame on one side. Pull each one taut across the top before nailing it to the opposite side of the frame on the underside of the stool.

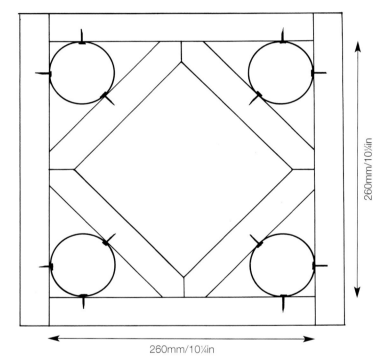

260mm/10¼in

260mm/10¼in

The underside of the stool

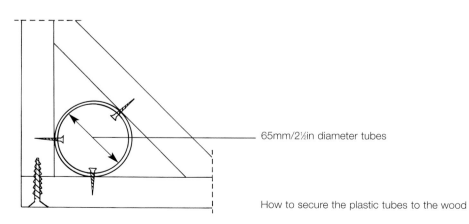

65mm/2½in diameter tubes

How to secure the plastic tubes to the wood

# kitchen wall organizer

This kitchen organizer is quick and easy to make. It's a way of expressing your personality, of displaying your favourite cooking or cleaning tools and of making more of the space in your kitchen. If you look in the right place for your materials it won't cost anything to make.

This project will particularly suit anyone who is on a budget, such as shared student houses, or short-term make-overs, and the measurements can be adapted to fit any space. Make one for above the sink and another with a shelf above and a row of hooks for mugs, or have one running the length of your work tops.

Choose brightly coloured plastic containers to cut down. The wooden framework could be painted to contrast with or match your colour scheme. This might mean switching brands or taking an unusual interest in the products under your friends' sinks for a while to get your hands on the best colour containers, but it will be worth it.

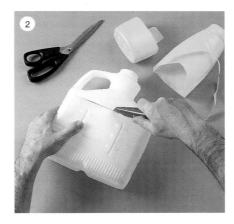

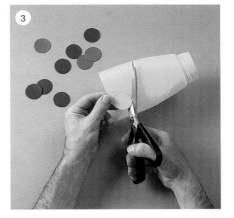

## cutting list

outer vertical backing wood x 2:
  320mm/12½in height/65mm/2½in width/10mm/½in depth

inner vertical backing wood x 2:
  320mm/12½in height/45mm/1¾in wide/10mm/½in depth

horizontal lengths of wood x 4:
  50mm/2in height/720mm/28½in width/10mm/½in depth

longer pieces to make the rack x 2:
  50mm/2in height/285mm/11¼in length/10mm/½in depth

short pieces to fit in between the rack x 2: 50mm/2in height/45mm/1¾in width/10mm/½in depth

## you will need

handsaw

sandpaper

selection of coloured plastic bottles – softener, dish-washing, orange juice

utility knife

scissors

compass

masking tape

drill, screws and screw cups

wood glue

1 Cut the timber. You will need four long and four short pieces and one shorter piece for the knife rack.

2 Sand away any potential splinters. Cut off the top halves of the plastic bottles and containers. Keep the bottom parts for later use, cutting them so that the back edge is at least 50mm/2in higher than the front – this part will be attached to the frame.

3 Use the compass to draw circles and cut out plastic discs from the top sections to use as washers.

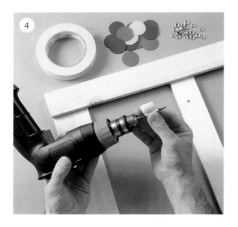

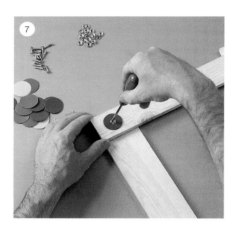

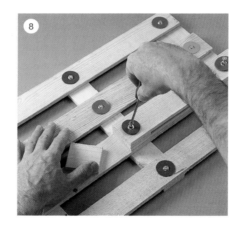

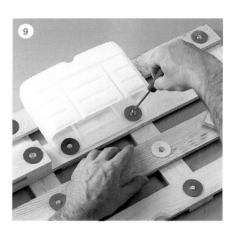

4 Measure the distance through the disc, the top piece of timber and just into the lower piece. Bind a piece of masking tape around the drill bit to limit the drilling depth.

5 Place some glue on a corner of a lower piece, position the top piece over it and add a coloured disc.

6 Drill through until you reach masking tape.

7 Place a screw cup over the hole and screw the parts together. Repeat on all four corners, then add the other pieces, except for the intersections where the knife rack fits.

8 To make a knife rack, cut two square spacers from the same timber. Cut a piece of timber one-third the length of the total width. Use longer screws but the same method to attach the knife rack.

9 Drill holes through the plastic back pieces and use the bright washers, screws and screw cups to attach them to the wooden grid. A large container like this will need two attachments.

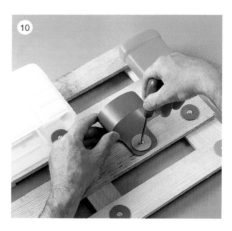

10 A single attachment is enough to secure smaller containers to the frame.

# woven lampshade

There are some really dull lampshades in the shops and malls and a glance around any charity, second-hand or thrift store will confirm this, as many end up there. Most lampshades are constructed on a similar type of metal frame, and the cover can be easily stripped away and replaced with something that pleases your eye.

Weaving is a creative activity with a rhythm that fits well with conversation and music – your fingers pick up the rhythm and, without realizing it, you work row after row and complete the pattern in no time at all. The only materials required for this project are an old lampshade

frame and a few metres/yards of electric flex (cord), which can be taken from any old household appliances and joined together as you weave.

The colours used here are those of standard cable, which is made up of brown-, green/yellow- and blue-coated copper wires, with some white light flex (cord). If you prefer, red, black, yellow or even the multicoloured computer or telephone wires could be woven with stunning results. The method remains the same, but the finer the wire the more rows you will need to cover the frame – and the more pleasure you will get from the making and the end result.

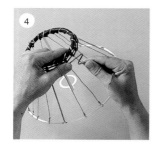

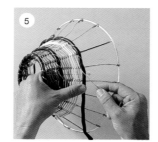

## you will need

old lampshade with a wire frame and the
  original cover removed
sandpaper
fine gauge galvanized wire
ruler
long-nosed pliers
wire cutters
black electric flex (cord)
2-strand white light flex (cord)
utility knife

1 Strip off the old lampshade covering and sand off any white paint on the three spokes which connect the two rings, to reveal the grey metal below it. Cut 15 equal lengths of galvanized wire to make extra spokes on the shade. Measure the height, then add about 40mm/1½in for twisting to secure them at top and bottom.

2 Slit open a length of black flex (cord) and remove the three coloured strands. Cut open the brown cable and remove the strands of copper wire.

3 Measure a piece of black cable casing to fit around the top of the frame. Secure the end of the copper wire by twisting it round one of the spokes, then press the black casing over the frame and bind it in place with the copper wire, spacing the twists of wire evenly around the cable casing.

4 Strip back the end of a blue cable and twist the copper around a spoke. Weave around the frame by taking the wire under the next spoke, then back and under it. Keep the wire as taut as possible and repeat until the blue is about 25mm/1in deep.

5 Bind a length of black cable casing on at this point, using the copper wire as before, then continue weaving, changing colours as you go.

6 Pull the double-stranded light flex (cord) apart and weave several white rows. Finish off the lampshade with another length of black casing, which should be pushed over the lower frame circle and bound on with the copper wire.

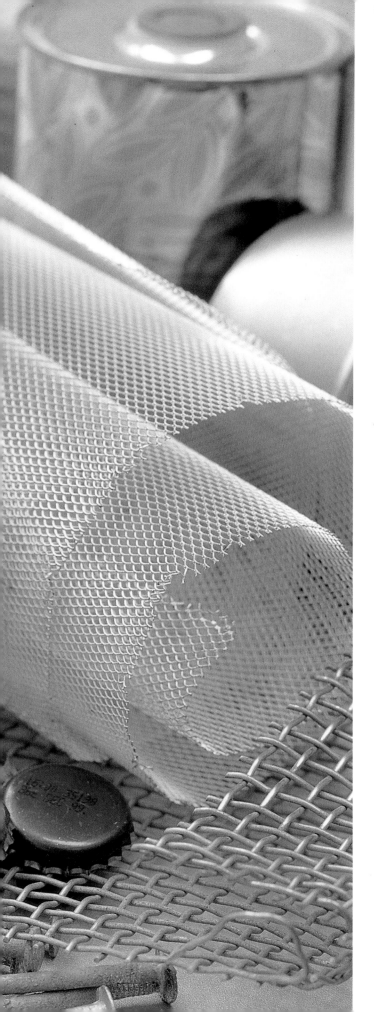

# metal

Metals are usually described by their worth, weight or properties, but in terms of scrap metal for recycled design work, they can be divided into categories like rusty iron, engine parts, chromed steel, enamelware and tin cans. Heavy metalwork demands a high skill level in a well-equipped workspace. Here, we have confined ourselves to making accessible domestic waste, like bottle caps and tin cans, into objects of utility and beauty.

*The talent on show here reveals a wide range of metalworking techniques. Some of these objects could not have been created without access to a well-equipped workshop, yet others required no more than a pair of wire snips and pliers. The hubcap only needed picking up from the roadside and fitting with hands and a battery mechanism and it was transformed into a stylish clock, whereas the giant cola bottle is a planned artwork. The bottle cap guitarist was made in a village in Africa and Rick Ladd's mirror (page 11) hails from Manhattan, yet both makers chose the same material for their creations.*

**Copper bowl** Peter Edwards is a prolific artist whose creative output is overwhelming. He is a compulsive collector and maker, and his favourite materials are recycled household plumbing appliances, such as this copper water tank. He has removed the domed top and cut a decorative edge to make a fabulous bowl, one of many on show in his gallery, where you can also see cistern ballcock and garden tool candelabra, melted plastic fruit bowls, lavatory seat chairs and hundreds of other quirky delights.

**Hubcap clock** This is another example of Peter Edwards' work. He prefers to use metal hubcaps, but this plastic one appealed to him because of the twelve holes, which suggested a perfect clock face. Peter disturbs the original surface of his found materials as little as possible, and the black holes are still coated with the carbon dust and oil that were there when he picked this up on the roadside.

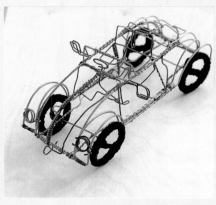

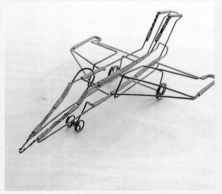

**Bottle cap man** This little guitar player, made in southern Africa, moves with the rhythm of the real thing. Pierced bottle caps have been threaded onto a wire body frame with a moveable crosspiece, which allows the arms to swing the guitar. This is part of a set of characters, which includes a kicking soccer player.

**Wire plane and car** The plane and car are examples of "factory-made" wire toys from South Africa. The designs are based on a style of toys made by township children. The originals were made in the spirit of soap box carts, with some element of competition among the children as to who could make the best, strongest, fastest and most cleverly articulated version. Tourists were fascinated by the ingenuity of the designs, and a market in replicas soon developed.

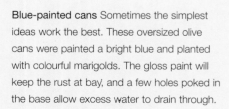

**Blue-painted cans** Sometimes the simplest ideas work the best. These oversized olive cans were painted a bright blue and planted with colourful marigolds. The gloss paint will keep the rust at bay, and a few holes poked in the base allow excess water to drain through.

**Funnel totem candlestick** An upturned galvanized metal funnel forms the base of this unusual candlestick, which has cut-out metal shapes slotted in and welded onto it. Its origin is unknown, but the effect is similar to a totem pole.

**Ray's car sofa** Ray McChrystal is an artist who usually paints large bright canvases. He could not resist turning his hand to furniture-making when his beloved Cortina was wrecked in an accident after years of painstaking restoration. Using an angle grinder to cut off the rear end, he put the back seat into the boot (trunk) and wired it up so that the tail lights can be turned on at night.

**Tin can flowerpots** Tea caddies and cocoa cans are used in a glorious display of summer flowers. This kind of recycling requires minimum effort but will add maximum character to a garden or patio.

**Oil lamp** This useful table lamp was made in India by a project that recycles metal. It was made from pink talcum powder cans and is filled from above. The tassel is a late addition, which is removed when the lamp is lit.

**Tin can holder** This charming little coffee-making set was made by the resident "metal man" in Crete, Greece. His workshop is a fascinating place, filled to the brim with everything from tractor parts for repair to delicate birdcages. He makes these sets from recycled food cans.

**Washing machine drum lamp** This standard lamp is made from the drum of a dismantled washing machine. It has a smart contemporary style and looks fabulous when it is lit, sending out hundreds of small beams of light. (Chris Richardson)

**Anchor** A huge rust-patinated anchor stands sentinel outside the front door of this converted chapel. Some utilitarian objects have such elegance that they are transformed into sculpture simply by being moved to an unlikely location.

**Old lamp** An old street light has, literally, been turned upside-down to make this smart steel uplighter.

**Coke bottle** This demonstrates Elisabeth's own unique form of Pop Art, transforming the waste product of a conglomerate culture into a tactile, six-foot structure constructed entirely from old cans. (Elisabeth Kaufmann)

**Strongbow** An abstract shiny wall hanging made from cutting up soft drinks cans and weaving and tying the aluminium strips together. (Elisabeth Kaufmann)

**Robostacker** A clever storage system using old washing machine drums designed by Jam in collaboration with appliance manufacturer Whirlpool. (Jam Design & Communications Ltd)

**Flat screen coffee tables** These coffee tables make use of old screens and have been adapted into useful contemporary furniture. These were designed by Jam in collaboration with Sony. (Jam Design & Communications Ltd)

**SineSeat public seating** This is the prototype of another project being undertaken by vk&c. It makes use of recycled cast aluminium and a product called Plaswood, which is processed from recycled agricultural polythene. The modular seating is very stylish, practical, hardwearing and easy to assemble. Moreover, not only is it made from recycled materials, but it is ultimately recyclable itself. (vk&c)

**Virgin Lips** The spectrum of colours of drinks cans means that there is a great deal of leeway in the creation of a piece of work with a colour scheme that suits the interior design needs of the client. "The never-ending variety of designs and innovative logos is my constant source of inspiration." (Elisabeth Kaufmann)

# using metal

Metal will always have served some useful purpose, and half the fun of working with it to recycle it is that we don't have the skills or facilities to alter its shape, so we have to incorporate that into our design. The fact that unrelated assembled components are recognizable is a large part of the new object's charm. While it is true that people with welding skills and equipment can take the recycling of metal into a different realm, those of us who own nothing more than a pair of work gloves, a pop riveter and a good pair of tin shears can also enjoy metalwork and make some wonderful things for our homes.

## Cutting and folding metal

1 Keep life as simple as possible by using the right tool for the job. A can opener will remove the top and base of any can in the neatest and safest possible way.

2 A pair of tin shears will cut through the seams of a tin can and leave slightly burred edges for safer handling. It is still advisable to wear a tough pair of work gloves when you cut metal.

3 Prepare a tin can for reuse by removing any folded seams with tin shears. The seams are more inclined to hold their original curves than a single sheet of tin.

  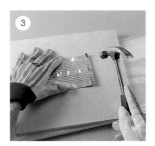

## Bending and straightening metal

1 To flatten a sheet of tin for reuse place it on a wooden board. Push it down against the curve and use a leather metalwork hammer to beat it flat.

2 To fold over the edge of a sheet of tin and provide a safe edge for handling, place the tin on a wooden board with the seam allowance overlapping, and use an ordinary hammer to flatten it over onto the edge of the board.

3 Once the edge is folded to a 90 degree angle, hold it firmly on a wooden board and flatten the seam with a hammer.

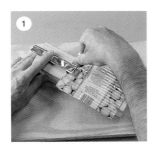  

## Riveting

1 Place the two pieces of tin to be joined on a piece of scrap timber and use a bradawl to make an indentation to guide the drill bit.

2 Hold the metal firmly and drill through both pieces of tin, using a 4.5 drill bit.

3 Place the rivet in the tool and position the end of the rivet in the hole. Apply pressure and, as you squeeze, the rivet will fit firmly into the hole and the two pieces will be joined.

## tools and equipment

**Work gloves** Wear heavy-duty gloves to protect your hands from sharp edges.

**Safety goggles** Impact-resistant plastic goggles or glasses should be worn whenever you cut metal.

**Hacksaw** A steel frame holds changeable blades that are suitable for cutting metal, ceramic tiles and glass.

**Tin snips** A small pair of snips is useful for making small cuts, such as when cutting wires, flex (cord) and cable.

**Tin shears** These are bigger and have spring-loaded handles for easy cutting. The bottom blade is serrated to improve grip and prevent distortion. It also leaves a slightly burred edge, which is safer to handle.

**Riveter** A riveter enables you to fix sheets of metal neatly together. It can also be used for other materials. A DIY (do-it-yourself) user's riveter will have slots for up to four sizes of rivet. They are inexpensive but extremely effective tools.

**Power drill** If you are using a riveter, a power drill is essential because rivet holes are pre-drilled. Metal is drilled with wood bits.

**Soldering iron** Although we did not use one in any of the projects, a soldering iron allows you to join small metal pieces.

**Hide hammer** This mallet-shaped hammer, with one copper end and one hide-covered end, is used for metalwork, where it is less likely to cause any damage when flattening thin metal sheets – tin cans, for instance. A soft-faced nylon and PVC hammer (rubber mallet) works in the same way.

# bottle cap mirror frame

Some things are too perfect to throw away, and this must have been the way bottle cap art began. In almost every country with an ethnic craft tradition and where resources are limited, people make things from bottle caps. As children, we collected them and nailed them to planks of wood in rows to make very efficient boot scrapers, or we threaded them on bent wire to make noisy percussion instruments.

One of the most stunning objects we have seen made from them was a huge throne, constructed from coils of thousands of caps by an American artist called Rick Ladd. This mirror frame is simplicity itself compared with his astonishing creations, but his work was our inspiration.

You would have to drink an awful lot of soda to make even one mirror, so we suggest that you ask your local café or bar to save bottle caps for you. As with any recycling project, the idea is to use up the materials you have available rather than investing in new ones. Adapt our measurements to suit your materials – the galvanized wire, for instance, can be any gauge that will thread through holes and give graceful curves, and the timber does not have to be the same width as ours, just of roughly similar proportions.

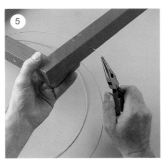
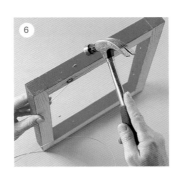

**1** Cut two pieces of timber, each 340mm/13½in long and two pieces, each 250mm/10in long. Place the shorter lengths inside the longer ones and mark screw positions on the outside edges with a bradawl. Place the timber flat on the workbench and drill the pilot holes for the screws. Glue the edges and screw together.

**2** Paint the frame using a bright coloured emulsion (latex) paint. We chose bright red emulsion (latex), but only a small amount of paint is needed, so use whatever you have to hand. Leave to dry.

**3** Place the bottle caps upside down on a piece of scrap timber and pierce them centrally using a narrow gauge nail and hammer. Leave sixteen unpierced; they will be used in a different way.

**4** Fit the drill with a fine drill bit (it should be slightly thicker than the gauge of the wire you are using). Drill through the frame from the outer to inner edges, 100mm/4in from each corner.

**5** Cut a length of wire, about 2m/6½ft, and poke the end through from the inside of the frame. Twist the end of the wire over on the outer edge with the pliers to form a small hook.

**6** Pull the wire through and secure it to the wooden frame by tapping the short end of the hook into the frame with a hammer.

**7** Thread the pierced caps onto the wire to form a curve across the corner.

**8** Push the wire through the outer edge of the frame, pulling it taut so that the caps press tightly against each other.

## you will need

prepared construction timber – about
  1.2m/4ft of 33 x 33mm/1⅓ x 1⅓in

pencil

ruler

handsaw

bradawl

3.5 drill bit

drill

countersink bit

wood glue

4 x 50mm/2in No. 8 screws

screwdriver

paint

paintbrush

about 1000 or more bottle caps

hammer

galvanized wire 1.5mm/⅟₁₆in diameter

long-nosed pliers

nails

**9** Thread twice the number of caps onto the wire for the outer curve. Push the wire through to the inner edge, pull it taut and thread again for the next inside corner curve. Continue this way until you have a coil of caps weaving in and out of the frame all the way round. Twist the end of the wire to form a stop knot and secure it to the frame with a one-inch nail.

**10** Cut four lengths of wire, 300mm/12in, and thread sixty bottle caps on each one. Twist the ends of the wire together to make circular shapes.

**11** Twist over the ends of sixteen lengths of wire, each 120mm/4¾in long, then thread ten caps on top of each other. Pierce more caps through the crimped top and bottom edges and thread the wire through so that the caps face forwards. Pull the wire taut and twist it behind the caps. Place four of these on each side at each corner or according to your design.

**12** Position a circle on each corner and use a bradawl to pierce a hole through the crimped edge of the cap and make a pilot hole in the frame.

**13** Place a pin in this hole and use a nail punch to hammer it home.

**14** Finally fill in any empty spaces on the front and sides of the frame using a hammer and pins to attach more bottle caps as desired.

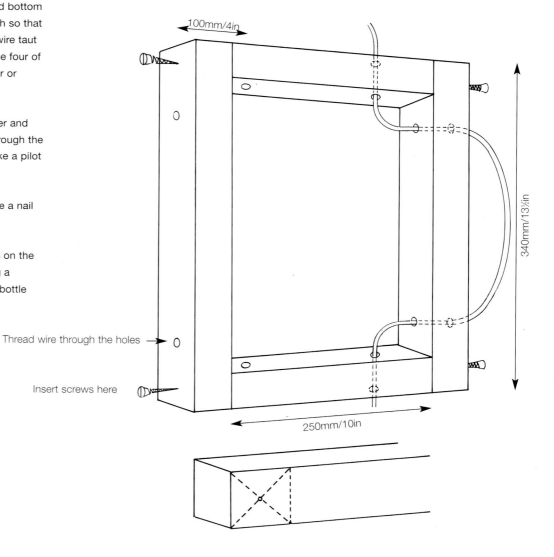

100mm/4in

340mm/13½in

250mm/10in

Thread wire through the holes

Insert screws here

# olive can lamp base

If you share our love affair with foreign packaging, you will want to get down to your nearest deli and persuade the owner to save you some giant olive cans. The olives that are sold loose by weight in delicatessens actually arrive in large, gloriously decorative, Italian or Greek cans, which beg to be on display somewhere.

Most shopkeepers are only too happy to find a taker for bulky refuse, so all that remains for you to do is to find the deli with the finest cans. The base of our lamp was made from one of these large olive cans, and the top section is a regular size supermarket can. The cans are used upside down because people always open them from the top; if this bothers you, ask the shopkeeper to make an exception and open a couple of cans the other way up.

Other good sources of large tins are restaurants, especially Indian, Greek or Chinese ones, where bulk-bought ingredients are often imported in distinctively foreign packaging with unusually bold colour combinations, exotic addresses and imprinted letters or numerals.

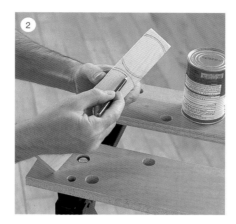

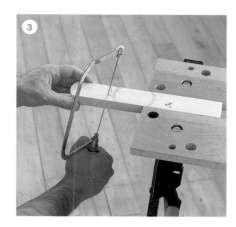

## you will need

olive can – ours contained 400g/14oz of olives

scraps of 25 x 12mm/2 x 1in construction timber

pencil

coping saw

catering size can – ours contained 300g/6½lb 9.8oz of olives

lamp fitting

bradawl

screwdriver

drill

4 x 10mm/⅜in brass screws and No. 2 bit, to attach lamp fitting

cable (cable holes need No. 7 bit) and plug

rubber grommit

**1** To make the two wooden fixing blocks that fit inside the top tin, stand the small tin on the timber and use a pencil to draw the circumference in two positions. The tin will overlap the timber, so just draw the points that touch.

**2** Draw an inner circle 3mm/⅛in inside this line to allow for the rim.

**3** Clamp the wood to a workbench and cut out the blocks to the inner line with a coping saw.

**4** Mark the position for the block on the top of the large can, then drill two holes to take the screws.

**5** Clamp an off-cut of timber vertically to the workbench or vice, put the top fixing block inside the smaller can and place the can over the upright timber. Centre the lamp fitting mounting plate on the base of the tin and mark the positions for the screws with a bradawl, piercing both the tin base and the wooden fixing block.

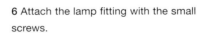

6 Attach the lamp fitting with the small screws.

7 Insert the lower fixing block into the smaller tin and make guiding holes through the sides of the tin. Drill pilot holes through the tin to the wood and screw up tightly.

8 Use a No. 7 or No. 8 bit to drill the cable hole through the top and base of the small tin, the top of the larger tin and near the base of the larger tin for the cable to exit.

9 Feed the cable through the holes. Fix the base to the top by screwing from the inside of the large tin up into the wooden block in the small tin.

10 Insert the grommit into the cable exit hole and push the cable up through the top of the lamp base to be connected with the lamp fitting.

# drinks can chandelier

Even if you have always recycled your cans, it still seems a waste of a lot of design effort when they are crushed flat. This chandelier is for sentimentalists who find small, colourful cans appealing. If you like the shape but don't have the packaging bug, you could make it anyway and add a coat of paint.

Small mixer cans are made from very light, soft metal alloys, and they can be cut with a utility knife or even a strong pair of scissors, but the brackets are made from a heavier metal, so tin snips will be necessary.

If you wonder about justifying the expense of buying the tin snips to make just one chandelier, don't – all your friends will want you to make them one, and the snips will get plenty of use. When they cut, they leave a less sharp, burred edge, which is safer to handle. You will undoubtedly find other uses for old cans too.

**1** Use a utility knife to cut the cups from the bottom of the small cans. They should be at least 30mm/1¼in deep.

**2** Remove the sharp edges with the tin snips, cutting each cup down to a depth of 25mm/1in.

**3** Place the piece of dowel in the centre of the cup base and tap it with a hammer to flatten the concave surface.

**4** Prepare the centre piece by cutting the larger tin down to the depth of 20mm/¾in.

**5** Follow the technique shown on page 137 to fold the edges and make the following strips of tin from a large oil can: eight strips each measuring 14 x 155mm/½ x 6in and four strips each measuring 14 x 235mm/ ½ x 9¼in.

**6** Clamp the scrap length of dowel to the workbench and gently tap the lengths of tin over it with a hammer to form the curves. A leather hammer is the ideal tool for this job. Work slowly with a small tapping motion to avoid getting hard angles.

## you will need

utility knife

13 individual mixer cans – tonic, soda, bitter lemon and so on

tin snips

off-cut of 20mm/¾in dowel or broom handle

hammer

other tin – ours has a 85mm/3½in diameter cut to 20mm/¾in deep

large can for bracket strips – ours was for olives

bradawl

pop riveter

4mm/⅛in aluminium short rivets

4mm/⅛in washers

drill

4.5mm/³⁄₁₆in drill bit suitable for metal

length of strong wire – a coat hanger is fine

50mm/2in

Approximate size of
candle holders

25mm/1in

85mm/3½in

20mm/¾in

Join the hanging sections like this

155mm/6in

10mm/⅜in

70mm/2¾in

110mm/4⅜in

235mm/9¼in

75mm/3in

165mm/6½in

View side on when constructed

tea light cups

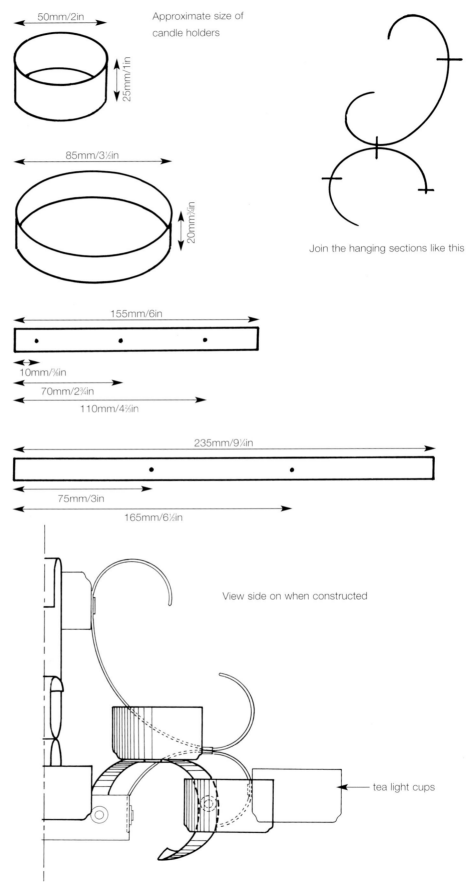

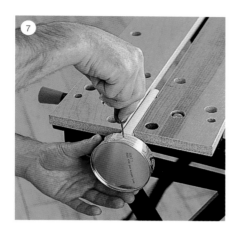

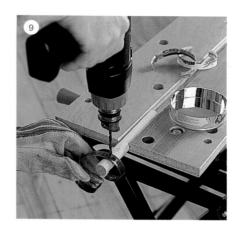

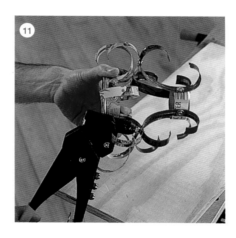

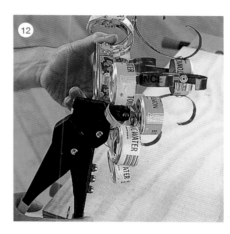

**7** Fix a piece of dowel into the jaws of the workbench so that it protrudes by 38mm/1½in. Mark the four cardinal points of the tin, then bisect the distance between them. Hold the tin over the curve of the dowel and use a bradawl to pierce 8 points to align with these marks. Make four pilot holes with a bradawl about 10mm/⅜in from the tin base at equidistant points.

**8** Make pilot holes 10mm/⅜in from the base on eight candle holders and four equidistant holes on the top ring. Make pilot holes in the centre of the base of four candle holders.

**9** Drill all pilot holes, including those in the curved support strips, with a 4.5mm/ ⁄in bit.

**10** Attach the top supports to top ring. (See riveting instructions in general metalwork section, page 137.)

**11** Assemble the lower supports to the lower ring and join together.

**12** Rivet the candle holders to the supports and punch a hole in the top ring to take the wire hanger.

**13** Twist a knot into one end of the wire, thread it through, then make a loop at the top to hang it up.

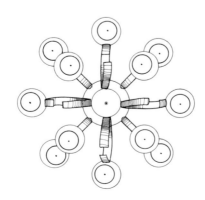

Overhead view

# kitchen drawer front

The beer market is highly competitive, and the designs on cans have to be uniquely attractive if one brand is to outsell its rivals. The result is great graphic design, far too good for the crusher, which can be used to give kitchen cabinets a make-over.

Drinks cans are easily cut with a strong knife, kitchen scissors or, ideally, tin snips. Cut aluminium has sharp edges, so we suggest that you wear work gloves for this stage. Tin could be fitted directly onto an existing drawer front or attached to thin plywood, which can later be attached to the drawer.

Invest in a set of new handles to go with the new look. We found a cheap set of chrome handles that suited the cans perfectly. We adapted them by fitting bolts with longer shafts to clear the thickness of the drawer, plywood and tin.

You can adapt this method to cover many surfaces and really go to town on the look.

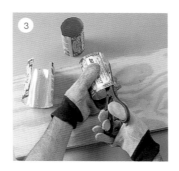

**1** Measure the drawer front and cut a piece of plywood or hardboard to match the size. Sand the edges smooth.

**2** Cut off the two ends of the cans using a craft knife. Drinks (beverage) cans are made from thin, soft material and are easily cut.

**3** Cut along the join (seam) of the tube with a pair of strong scissors.

**4** To flatten the metal, hold a piece of wood firmly on it with one hand and pull it through with the other.

## you will need

plywood or hardboard
sandpaper
beer or soft drinks cans, about five
work gloves
craft knife
tin snips
strong scissors
felt-tip pen
drill with 4.5mm/³⁄₁₆in bit
pop riveter and rivets
screwdriver
metal straightedge
panel adhesive
handle with long bolts

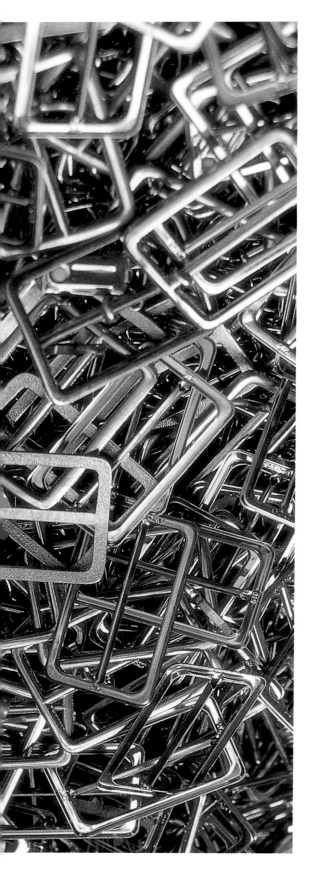

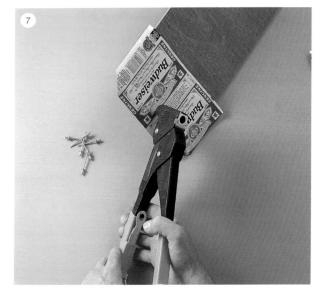

**5** Place one flat sheet of tin face down on a wooden board and place one end of the plywood on top so that an equal amount of tin overlaps all around. Draw the shape onto the can with a felt-tip pen.

**6** Cut away the corners, then position the metal on the panel. Drill holes to take the rivets; one at the top, one at the bottom. Use a 4.5 bit to drill the three equally spaced 4mm holes.

**7** Fit the rivets and then use the riveter to press them into place. Do the same with another flat sheet for the other end. Place another flat sheet of tin face down on a wooden board and score a line 10mm/½in from the edge with a screwdriver and metal straightedge.

**8** Hold a piece of straightedged scrap timber along the line and use a hammer to flatten the scored section against it. Remove the timber and hammer the seam flat. Make enough of these safe-edged can strips to fill in the centre of the drawer front. Wrap the strips around the drawer edges, top and bottom, and rivet them in place. Use a piece of scrap timber to fold and flatten the tin over onto the back of the panel.

**9** Fit the handle in the middle of the drawer front, drilling the appropriate holes to secure it. Note the depth of the drawer and panel and choose a handle with sufficient bolt length.

# templates

The measurements given are those used within the individual projects. For an enlargement, either use a grid system or photocopier.

You can alter these measurements to suit your needs but be sure to change all measurements in proportion.

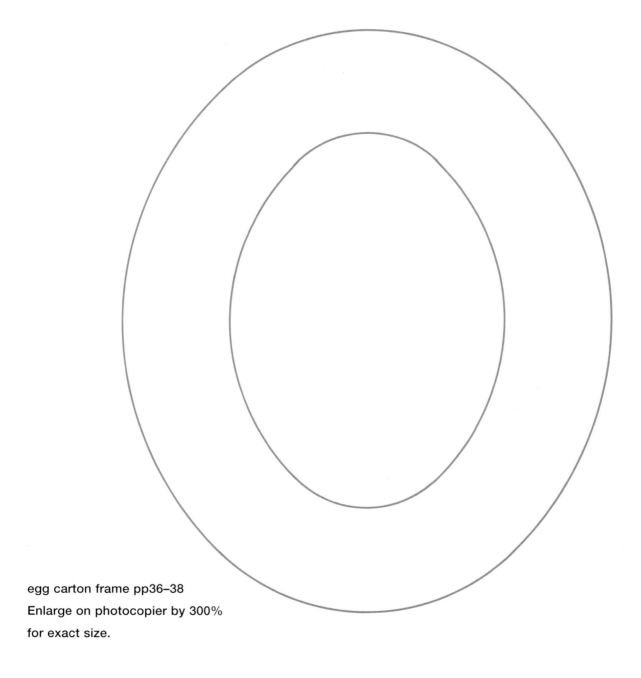

**egg carton frame pp36–38**
**Enlarge on photocopier by 300%**
**for exact size.**

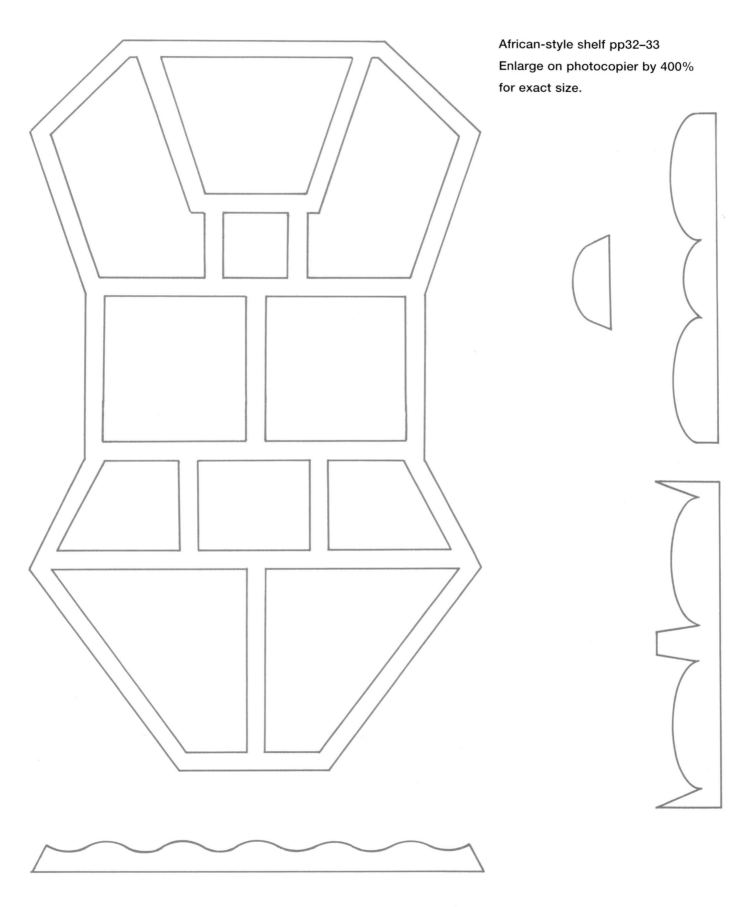

**African-style shelf pp32–33**
Enlarge on photocopier by 400%
for exact size.

# useful addresses

## United Kingdom

Architectural Salvage
30-32 Stamford Road
London N1 4JL
Tel: 0207 923 0783
*Architectural salvage yard*

Brats
624c Fulham Road
Parsons Green
London SW6 5RS
0207 731 6915
*Suppliers of Mediterranean paints*

Children's Scrap Project
137 Homerton High Street
Hackney
London E8
Tel: 0208 985 6290
*Suppliers of waste materials to
institutions*

Janine Tutt
Ashwell Recycling
Unit 9, Criton Industrial Estate
Stanford Road
Orsett
Essex
Tel 01375 892576
*Recycled timber supplier*

Architectural Rescue
47 Southampton Way
London SE5
Tel: 020 7277 0315
*Architectural salvage yard*

Churchills Architectural Salvage
212 Old Kent Road
London SE1
*Architectural salvage yard*

The Reclamation Association
P.O.Box 124
6 Storey's Gate
London SW1P 3AU
*Information on textile recycling
network*

Waste Watch
Gresham House
24 Holborn Viaduct
London EC1A 2BN
0870 243 0136
*Listings of scrap materials projects
plus all kinds of recycling information*

British Glass Recyling Company Ltd
Northumberland Road
Sheffield S10 2UA
0114 268 6201
*Information on glass recycling*

Friends of the Earth
26-28 Underwood Street
London N1 7JQ
0207 490 1555
www.foe.co.uk

Crafts
The Crafts Council Magazine
44a Pentonville Road
London N1 9BY
0207 278 7700
www.craftscouncil.org.uk

Raw Vision
42 Llanvanor Road
London NW2 2AP
*International contemporary folk art
and Outsider Art magazine*

Salvo magazine
Ford Village
Berwick-upon-Tweed
TD15 2QG
www.salvo.co.uk
*Architectural salvage news plus
address lists of salvage yards
countrywide*

RECOUP
9 Metro Centre
Welbeck Way
Woodston
Peterborough
Cambridgeshire PE2 7WH
01733 390021
www.recoup.org/recoup
*Information on plastic recycling
projects, companies and contacts*

## United States

Dick Blick Art Materials
P.O. Box 1267
695 US Highway 150 East
Galesburg, IL 61402
www.dickblick.com
*Suppliers of art and craft materials*

Craft King
P.O. Box 90637
Lakeland, FL 33804
Tel: (800) 769-9494
www.craft-king.com

The Jerry's Catalog
P.O. Box 58638
Raleigh, NC 27658
Tel: (800) U-ARTIST
www.jerryscatalog.com
*Art and design suppliers*

Art Supply Warehouse
5325 Departure Drive
North Raleigh, NC 27616
Tel: (919) 878-5077
www.aswexpress.com

Craft Catalog
P.O. Box 1069
Reynoldsburg, OH 43068
Tel: (800) 777-1442

Woodcrafts and Supplies
405 East Indiana Street
Oblong, IL 62449
Tel: (800) 592-4907
www. woodcraftssupplies.com

Recycler's World
www.recycle.net
*Recycling information internet site*

Earth's 911
www.1800cleanup.org
*Environmental and recycling
information site*

Environmental Health Center
1025 Connecticut Avenue, NW,
Suite 1200
Washington, DC 20036
Tel: (202) 293-2270
Fax: (202) 463-2471
*A division of the National Safety
Council*

Raw Vision
163 Amsterdam Avenue
203 New York
NY 10023-5001, USA
www.rawvision.com
INFO@afandpa.org
*International contemporary folk art
and Outsider Art magazine*

National Recycling Coalition
1727 King Street, Suite 105
Alexandria, VA 22314
Tel: (703) 683-9025
Fax: (703) 683-9026

## Bibliography

*Contemporary American Folk Art –
A Collector's Guide.* Chuck & Jan
Rosenak (Abbeyville Press, 1996)

*Perspectives on American Furniture.*
Gerald W.R. Ward (W.W. Norton & Co.,
1988)

*American Folk Masters.* Steve Sporin
(Harry N. Abrams Inc., 1992)

*Trashformations.* Lloyd E. Herman
(University of Washington Press, 1998)

*Don't Throw it All Away.* Friends of the
Earth publication (New Edition, 1998)

*Recycled, Re-seen.* Crafts Council
Exhibition Catalogue (Cernry & Seriff)

*Raw Vision Magazine.* A quarterly
magazine published by Raw Vision Ltd.
website: www.rawvision.com

# index

# acknowledgements

There are so many talented artists and designers working with recycled materials now and the authors and publisher are delighted to have the chance to showcase some of them in this book. A special thank you to Chris Richardson and Gill Alcock for allowing us into their home in Rye; to Ray McChrystal for allowing us to show the world his Cortina settee; to Simon Brown for the use of his chapel as a photographic location; to the Filo pub for saving all those bottle caps; to the Hackney Scrap project for allowing us to photograph some of their bounty; to Spike Powell for his stunningly beautiful pictures; to the stylist Andrea Spencer for her creative styling; to Rodney Forte for his excellent step-by-step shots, to Joanna Lorenz for believing in the idea and to Doreen Palamartschuk for staying calm. A big thank you to those who contributed their work and apologies to those we didn't have room for and for those we didn't find.

Ben Hall
26a Fransfield Road
Sydenham
London SE26 6BA

Elisabeth Kaufmann
11 Great Russell Mansions
Great Russell Street
London WC1B 3BE

Andrea Peters
The Pea Green pottery
Greenman Street
Islington
London N1 8SE
020 7359 5646

Kristy Wyatt-Smith
99a Newington Green Road
London N1 4QY
020 7354 8355

Joseph O'Connor
5b Station Road
Middlesex TW1 4LL
020 8892 9363

Peter Edwards
Sow's Ear Gallery
George Street
Old Town
Hastings TN35 5AZ

Rory and Fiona Dodd
Same
146 Brick Lane
London E1

vk&c partnership
2/2 248 Woodland Road
Glasgow G3 6ND
0141 332 2049

Ralph Jessop
21 Norman Road
Sutton
Surrey SM1 2TB

Idonia van der Bijl
25A Museum Street
London WC1 1JT

Elizabeth Beesley
26 Kirby Road
Coventry
West Midlands CV5 6HN

Mary Hooper
26 Meadow Crescent
Bexhill
East Sussex TN39 5AR

Chris Richardson and Gill Alcock
The Workhouse
Cinque Port Street
Rye TN31 7AD

Vanessa Godfrey
9 Beehive Green
Welwyn Garden City
Herts AL7 4BE
01707 324708

Jam Design & Communications Ltd
2nd Floor
1 Goodsway
London NW1 1UR
020 7278 5567